What Was I Thinking

Thoughts

Emile Fougere

Contents

INTRODUCTION TO WHAT WAS I THINKING

I have been writing these thoughts for over two years now. It started because of Corona Virus as you can tell by my first few thoughts. There's only so much that can be said on that subject that hasn't already been said. I had to stop, even I was getting bored with the subject. I started enjoying what I was doing, so I kept going. To date I've written quite a few of these thoughts. I've been told by many that some of these thoughts are entertaining, informative, philosophical and funny. Even the word "hilarious" was used once, and "I laughed my ass off" was used once. I think he may have been exaggerating because the next time I saw him he still had an ass. Sometimes when I reread some of them it even makes me laugh. I think I saw a smile on my girlfriend's face once. Just kidding. If I can make a difference or put a smile on just one person's face it would make me happy.

My new goal is to turn these thoughts into a book. If you are reading this, "I did it." I know, a bit lofty but hopefully doable. Dreams can come true. I can do this. "Think positive." This is me talking to myself, that's alright, right? As long as I don't answer back I'll be fine. Right??

This book has many topics under THOUGHTS and MINI-THOUGHTS. It has jokes, it has anecdotes, it even has poems.

— Emile (thinking positive) Fougere

WHAT TO BELIEVE, WHAT NOT TO BELIEVE – THAT IS THE QUESTION

Too bad we don't have Archie Bunker & the Meathead to debate this. We might get better results.

Many doctors say that we should take the vaccine and many say we shouldn't. Who is right? Some doctors say it will boost your immune system and some say it will destroy your immune system. Who is right? Some say someone came out with the vaccines too quickly and some say that they have been working on them for decades. Who is lying? I read that the Pfizer vaccine was originally designed for rabbits in 2008. Is this true? I don't know. Maybe just another lie?

They say that most of the people that enter the hospital that die from *whatever* and they aren't vaccinated, then they blame it on corona virus. Another lie?

When the vaccine first came out I didn't want it. I have a very strong immune system. I've had very few colds or flus in thirty years and I've never had a flu shot. But with all the news coverage and doctors reports (mine included) I got the Corona Virus shots.

First one, mild side effects. The second, not so mild. I heard music in my head. Just FM, lots of country music. I had to install a volume control button on my left nipple and a tuning button on my right nipple. (*Just kidding*)

I have a feeling I'm gonna wish I hadn't gotten the vaccine, if my immune system is compromised. I won't be able to sue all the doctors who might have lied. With all these doctors and scientist in the world you would think it would have been possible for them all to have gotten together to decide on one plan of action and say this is it. Let's stop all this **BULL SHIT. ENOUGH IS ENOUGH.**

— Emile (*I can't take any more*) Fougere

FOOD FOR THOUGHT

Have you ever thrown your back out? I have a few times in my life. Do you know what I have learned from my experiences? Do you want to know? No! I'll tell you anyway. The first few times I spent twenty to thirty dollars on different things to help take the pain away. And each time it took two week for the pain to go away. I found out if you do nothing it still takes two weeks for the pain to go away. Well, I learned a better and cheaper way to get rid of the pain and to keep it away, believe it or not. Acupressure. It works like a charm. Lesson learned and money saved. It works for many other things too. Memory, E.D., you name it, even colds and flus. It doesn't say anything about corona virus. These books were written BCV (before corona virus). And the best thing is, you can do it all on yourself. FREE.

It was the same thing when I use to catch a cold or a flue, I would take all kinds of meds and I would buy all kinds of drugs and it would take a couple of weeks to get better. So the next time I got a cold or a flu and did nothing and guess what, in two weeks I felt better and I saved money.

Like I said in (Thought #1) I did get vaccines # 1, 2 & 3 reluctantly. And maybe at the cost of my immune system, (I hope not). I've had two heart attacks and I'm diabetic (not because of the vaccine). So if these vaccines have compromised my immune system like some say and I was to catch the virus I'm SCREWED. So should I keep away from people who have been vaccinated? (who may or may not be carriers) or people who are not vaccinated and (may or may not be carriers). I don't know. If I do catch the virus maybe I'll just wait two weeks and wait for it to go away. For extra protection I'll just take vitamin D and do acupressure for cold and flu for added protection. Can never be too careful. Just saying.

— Emile (Here's hoping) Fougere

DRUGS

Have you been to a pharmacy lately? There are so many drugs in there for so many different things. It's hard to keep up to all of them. There are more commercials on TV for drugs than anything else. How many ways can you cure Constipation and Diarrhea anyway and how big a problem is it? Shit, I don't know. You tell me. And Diarrhea, don't get me started, really , don't get me started. Now thats a crappy subject. Stop eating food that make you go, if you know what I mean. Do I have to spell it out for you. I better not. I could get sued.

One hundred year ago if someone had rode into town with all the concoctions they have today they would have been tarred and feathered or beaten half to death or both. Now, look what has happened. They say, look at all the wonderful drugs man has invented and yet he hasn't even come up with a cure for the common cold or flue. Gee, I wonder what would happen today if someone said they had a Vaccine for the cold? "What another Vaccine, you're not going to try that on me." People were mad because they had to wear masks and yet how many flus and colds did you hear about that year? Is it possible that Corona Virus cured the common cold and flue. Just saying. Well, it didn't cure it, it just taught us that if we wear masks and social distance during flu season we won't catch the flu or a cold.

Did you know that because of the Corona Virus water and air pollution dropped drastically, but only because there was less traffic on the roads and in the air, but on the down side there was more crime and violence, domestic and otherwise. Not much of a trade off. Go figure.

— Emile (*Just the messenger*) Fougere

MASKS OR NO MASKS

I don't call these thoughts of the day because I don't have them every day. It would hurt my brain too much. Should we wear masks or not? That is the question. Before Corona Virus I met a woman at one of the places where I worked who wore a mask every day for years because she was allergic to most smells in and around her. And some people smelled pretty bad, perfume wise. The big question is which was worse for her the smells or wearing the mask? In her case it was the smells. I heard of a man on facebook say that wearing a mask was dangerous because breathing in your own carbon dioxide is not good for you. Makes sense I guess. **Not**. But is it worse than breathing in Corona Virus? I don't think so. So, anyway he tried to prove his point by taking a monitoring devise from where he worked that could check dangerous levels of toxins and he hooked a tube to his face mask and an alarm went off to show that inhaling your own breath was dangerous. He must have had pretty bad breath. I think if he had gone to the bathroom and farted he probably had gotten the same results. Does that mean we should ban farting? Which also means his wife should use a mask whenever he uses the bathroom.. Another thing, if he was to walk down the chemical isle of any grocery store he would get the same results. So it's probably a good idea that we wear masks when we do our shopping. If wearing a mask is so bad why do doctors and nurses live so long. They wear masks every day and they live just as long as the rest of us.

— Emile (Don't hold your breath) Fougere

RELIGION OR ALIENS

Which do you believe in? I'm like the man who was asked which religion he believed in and he answered, all of them. It's good to leave your options opened. Better to be safe than sorry. I've read the Bible a few times and I've made a study of it for a few years and it does have it's merits. I've read a lot of books and I've seen a lot of documentaries on UFO's and aliens. The thing is, I've never seen UFO's or aliens, by the same token I've never seen God. If they both exist I'm not 100% sure, are you? Is anyone? Here's a good question. Did God create aliens (if they do exist) or did aliens create the idea of God? This has been suggested by many.

I have been watching a lot of Ancient Alien shows and there's a lot to be said for all the proof that there is all over the world, showing that aliens have been here since the dawn of time, even during bible times. Is it the devil or is it aliens? Would God let the devil go to all those lengths to fool so many people. Think about it. Sorry to say. It's enough to convince the most devout christian. Thousands of UFO's, Pyramids made to transmit signals to outer space, little grey men, crop circles, the list goes on and on.

Like I said at the beginning, I don't know if God created Aliens or Aliens created God. I'm flexible. Better to be safe than sorry.

If one or the other comes knocking at my door, I'll probably shit my pants. Just saying.

— Emile (*Take me to your leader*) Fougere

WHAT TO DO? WHAT TO DO?

I'll start with a little history about myself... I was born Sept. 26,1948 — Just kidding. Fast forward (July 2019). I had been working at my business for over 30 years and my health had started to deteriorate and had gotten worst for some time. My partner, her daughter and her grandson were doing all my work for me. I had gone from 125 lbs to 100 lbs, so in February of 2020 I sold my business and I retired, one month before the corona virus started. Hence the question "*What to do, what to do?*" I started eating more, I started exercising and I started having a more positive attitude and slowly but surely I got better. Now I weight 150 lbs.

Now, like everyone else I was in the middle of the virus with nothing to do and nowhere to go. I was hoping when I retired that I would be able to play golf, play my guitar and do a lot more karaoke and travel. Because of my damaged left hand, I couldn't play golf or guitar and because of the virus I couldn't go out to karaoke and no travel. We (Noella and I)bought a mini van with a mattress in it and we were hoping to drive across Canada. No such luck. Maybe next year.

In the meantime, in between time (*I think there's a song in* there somewhere), to pass the time. I exercised two hours a day for my heart. For my brain I read. Did you know that if you read novels it exercises a certain part of your brain unlike television and if you read books on medicine or science it exercises another part of your brain (*just a side note*). Doing this helps you avoid Alzheimer's. Over the years I've written a few poems and a few songs, which made me feel good. Now I feel that doing **this** also makes me feel good. Now I know "*What to do, what to do?*" What are you doing to make you feel good?

— Emile (*If you're not moving forward your standing still*)
Fougere

SAVE THE MOSQUITOS

I was washing my van the other day and I noticed how many dead mosquitos there were on the front of my van and on the mirrors and it made me think. With all the cars and trucks in the world that are traveling on the highways everyday how come mosquitos have not become extinct? And why are they not on the endangered species list? Actually, who would even want to see the mosquitos to go extinct? I wonder if I could apply to the government for a million dollar grant to do a study to help the mosquitos? Maybe I could go one better. I could get a rally together. Get as many people as possible to drive to Ottawa to protest against all those cars and trucks on the highways, Whoops, that would be self defeating. We would have to march to Ottawa. Let's pick a date. How about July 15, 2022? By the way if you decide to go, bring your mask, walk six feet apart and bring your vaccination card and don't forget your mosquito repellant. Just kidding , maybe. I posted this a couple of years ago, I hope it wasn't this post that gave the truck drivers the idea to drive to Ottawa for their protest, Sorry! Maybe.

I have an idea, lets do like the Chinese and ride bicycles. Bring signs (Save the Mosquitos).

It's been two years since I wrote this and the mosquitoes haven't gone extinct yet so lets put this on hold for now. We can try again in five years if *we* haven't gone extinct first.

Have you ever wondered why Noah didn't swat the two mosquitoes on the arc? I wish we could at least crossbreed the mosquitoes and the lightning bugs so we could see them coming at night.

— Emile (*Here's hoping*) Fougere

OH, LORD IT'S HARD TO BE HUMBLE

There was this man (this is not a fable, you know who you are) probably a good man, a humble man. He wanted to do good for his country. He was well known, well educated. He thought he would become a politician to lead his country. He had good intentions in the beginning and everybody liked him. He even said if he became the head of this country it would not change him. He would continue to take the bus to work or ride his bike (sometimes). My, how things have changed. He has a limo and a jet to take him everywhere, a big house, a cottage bigger than the apartment building I live in that he spent over 1 million dollars to fix up. Not so humble now.

If you are thinking of becoming a politician, think hard and long about it. It's true. Money and power do corrupt, no ifs ands or buts about it. If you know someone that you like, that is running for some kind of office (and it doesn't have to be political) do them a favor, don't vote for them for their own sake. It's hard enough to be the head of your own household never mind the head of a country, without it going to your head. Yes, it is hard to be humble and I'm not perfect in any way either. Have you figured out who I was talking about? His initials are J.T.

— Emile (*Did I say that out loud?*) Fougere

MY FAVORITE PAST TIME - DREAMING

Try not to fall asleep while you read this because that would be ironic. What is dreaming? Why do we dream? What is the purpose of dreaming? So many questions so few answers.

When I met Noella she told me she didn't dream and after we started living together she started dreaming. I guess I wasn't her dream come true after all. Just kidding Noella (maybe). Anyway, back to the subject at hand. Many people have written books on the subject of dreams and their meaning.

I don't know if there based on science, science fiction or opinion , but whatever. I've heard that if your dreaming that your flying (like superman) its sexual and you might have a wet dream. Does that mean if you have a dream about sex you might get air sick. Just a thought. At my age I live for dreams. Why, you may ask? Have you ever visited someone in a nursing home? A friend or a relative? If you have you might have seen a lot of people sitting in chairs in front of the TV, asleep. They are probably dreaming. When I was young I dreamt, but I didn't think much about my dreams then, except when I dreamt about flying. I don't dream much about flying anymore, boo hoo. Sorry, I digress. Anyway, now that I'm retired and I can't do much because of Covid, life can be pretty boring. I don't sleep a lot, but when I do I dream. I like dreaming now (most nights) except when I dream about work . At my age now, I don't see too many people I know, either their dead, moved away because of that damn Covid.

On the plus side, when I dream I can dream about just about anyone I want. Friends, old and new. People on facebook say they miss their dead loved ones (don't take this the wrong way) I do miss them but I don't. I see them in my dreams whenever I want to. As a matter of fact, more often than I use to when I was alive because I was too busy working.. To me they are still alive (in my dreams). My dreams seem so vivid and real like I can touch them and feel them (especially the old girlfriends). It's not like reliving the past, but more like making new memories, memories I couldn't make when they were alive.When I was working, sometimes eight days a week, I didn't have time to make these kind of memories. In my dreams, I'm still playing drums with my old friends, still hanging out with my old buddies and seeing my parents more often. During these days of Covid, weather your young or old, dream, it might be the only way to keep your sanity.

Are you still awake? If your not I hope your having a good dream.

It takes me a long time for me to write my thoughts. I have to do a lot of spell checking. When you have tremors you end up with more letters than you wantttt,,, see, just an example, that one was on purpose. And when you type with only one hand, in my case one finger (*you know the* one) it takes a lot longer. But it's fun. At my age you take fun where you can get it.

— Emile (*That was fun*) Fougere

MY BODY, MY CHOICE

Where do I start? In the last fifty years or so we have had to make so many choices or so it seems. And maybe even all through out history choices had to be made. But lets just talk about lately. First, lets talk about seat belts. Should we wear seat belts or not? Now that was a big one. Where did you stand (*Or should I say sit*)*?* Do you think we should have stop signs and traffic lights at intersections? I seen a video the other day of a town where there were no stop signs or traffic lights. I was surprised no one was killed. There were so many close calls though. In England they had a choice, should they drive on the right side of the road or the left. So what they did was for a week they had trucks drive on the left and the cars on the right. Then they would decide. *Just joking.* Now, here in Canada we drive on the right side. What if I decided one day I wanted to drive on the left, do I have that right? Is it my choice? Just asking.

In my life I have had many choices, many of which were wrong. Should I smoke? Should I drink? Should I gamble? Should I eat lots of candy? Should I drink & drive? Or all of the above like me? Not all of these things have consequences. Not every one who smokes gets cancer but the possibility is there. Not every one who drinks will ruin their liver but the possibility is there. Not everyone who eats a lot of junk food will get fat or get diabetes but the possibility is there. Not every one who drinks and drives will kill himself or someone else but the possibility is there. The list goes on and on. Its sad that governments have to make laws to protect us, but they do. Is it because we are stupid or we just don't care about others or ourselves. Sometimes it looks like both. Sorry. If I'm wrong tell me. If there were no traffic lights do you think everyone would act more cautiously? We have lights now and people are still running lights. There are warnings on cigarette packages and people still smoke. People want what they want, right or wrong.

Believe it or not my father told me that his doctor had told him that smoking was good for you. Can you believe that? I did. My mother was diabetic and now I wished she had drilled into me the importance of not eating too much junk food. As far as drinking an driving, I didn't always listen and I was lucky on so many levels. In a lot of these situations I felt it was better to be safe than sorry. It (could) be the same thing with Corona Virus. When it comes to Corona Virus we might look back at this in the same way.

— Emile (*Decisions, decisions*) Fougere

SPECIAL GIFTS

Do you have a special gift or gifts that you were born with? I think everyone has at least one. It could be you were a wiz at math in school or spelling. Just to name a couple. In school I was not very good at any subject, not to say that I didn't have a special gift. I guess that's not totally true. In gym I could hold my breath longer than anyone else. The other kids said I was probably breathing through my big ears. Yes, kids were cruel even back then.

Later on in life I found I had a natural talent for some of the arts. I was pretty good at drawing, but I never pursued it. Most of my younger years whenever I heard music I would bang on whatever I could put my hands on to the sound of music or play air guitar. When I was 19 I went to a dance and when the dance was over I asked the drummer if I could try his drums. He said yes, and the band started playing a song and I played the song all the way through. The drummer asked me how many years I've been playing. I told him it was the first time I had ever touched a set of drums. He could not believe it. That same night these four other guys were trying to start a band and one thing led to another and within a month or two I don't remember exactly, we were playing on that same stage.

Many years later and three bands later I was playing in this band in Moncton, keep in mind, I just played drums, but I would sing along (*no mike*) to every song. Picture this, New Years Eve, we're all set up and the lead singer calls the club where we were playing and tells us that he can't make it. His wife went into labour. What to do, what to do. Now the manager of the band could sing, but only 10 songs (Hank Williams). It's New Years Eve. Can't cancel. So I said, hook me up with a mike and a music stand and I'll sing. It turned out to be the best night ever and the lead singer never came back.

My point, everyone has a hidden talent.Whats yours. My girlfriend Noella has many gifts some of which I wish I had. I think if she could have pursued her education when she was younger she could have been a lawyer or a politician. She is not shy when it comes to speaking her mind. She has even put a few politicians in their place. I can sing in public but theres no way I can speak in public like her. There are people that are good sales people, not me, I tried it.

If you have a special talent that has come naturally to you or you know someone, I would like to hear about it. Even if your an alien from another planet, don't be shy. Send me an e-mail: emile1948@hotmail.com

— Emile (*Don't be shy*) Fougere

FARTS, GAS & DINOSAURS

In the beginning when dinosaurs roamed the earth, I can only imagine how messy things were. Dinosaurs were gigantic and there were probably lots of them and all kinds, so I've heard. Which means, you guessed it, lots of doo doo. With lots of doo doo means lots of methane gas. Now I would not want to be someone who is standing behind one of those giants when it farted. More methane.

The theory is that dinosaurs went extinct because of a large meteorite that hit the earth and wiped out the dinosaurs. I think thats only part of it. I think what really happened was a combination of a small meteorite and all that methane gas and *voila* "The Big Bang."

Which brings us to our present day. We are living in a world in which we have billions of cars, trucks, planes and boats that produce all kinds of methane gas, plus every animal in the world produces doo doo (methane gas) and us (humans) too. Plus politicians who are full of it too.. Maybe the next time they send a man into space *that* might ignite the next "Big Bang."

— Emile (*Up, up and away?*) Fougere

ADDICTIONS

Definition: The fact or condition of being addicted to a particular substance, thing or activity. Another definition: a biopsychosocial disorder characterized by compulsive engagement in re*warding stimuli despite adverse consequences*. (*That's a mouth full*). Have I lost you yet? Sorry.

I believe everyone has been or is addicted to something, (*believe it or not*) Ripply. When I was young I was addicted to television, to the point my parents had to kick me out of the house to go out and play Which was quite amazing considering back then (*in the olden days*) we only had two stations (*black & white*) at the time. Impossible you say. Well it's true.

Here are a few of the other things that are addictive, some obvious, some not so obvious.

Obvious: Drinking, Smoking, Drugs, gambling, spending money, and hoarding. As you may know by experience or noticed in others, these can be bad for your health, your finances or to the detriment of your family life.

Not so obvious: Puzzles, sex, the big M, playing games, (*Fun*) can be taken to extremes. Some of these can be a complete waste of time.

Example:

When video games first came out I tried Mario Brothers, at first my wife and I played for an hour, the next time we played for two hours, one night we were playing, the next thing we new it was morning. That was the last time we played. Can you see how things can get away from you? Gambling can get you the sane way. For anyone who is still gambling I have a simple test for you to help you quit. If your going to continue to gamble anyway try this. Every time you gamble, mark down on a piece of paper what you win or lose and at the end of the month add and subtract everything and see if your ahead or behind. Try that for as many months as you want to. After a while you'll find there are very few months that you are ahead, if any at all. Don't try it for too long you might end up in the poor house unless your already there. I can guarantee you there will never be a month that you will be ahead unless you are very lucky. Some things that are necessary can be addictive too. Can *work* really be called addictive? Was I a workaholic? I don't think so. When I retired I didn't go into withdrawal. Sure I still dream about work more often than I would like to, (*more often than sex*) that doesn't make me a workaholic, does it? Eating or exercising, but taken to an extreme, even these things can be addictive. Of all the things that are addictive, the worst I think is "MONEY." They say that money is the root of all evil but that's not true. The truth is, it's the desire or the love of money, that's the root of all evil. People kill for money, they steal for money, they have sex for money.

Even rich people, people who have millions of dollars will kill for more money, will even cheat poor people to get more. Can you imagine selling women and children into sex slavery for money. It does't get any worse than that.

We all have or had addictions in our lives, some bad some not so bad. The thing is, do we recognize them and are we willing to do something about them. Remember, keep the good ones and discard the bad ones and you'll be a better person for it. If your addiction isn't hurting yourself or anyone else then it's just a habit. So it's all right to keep watching Wheel of Fortune.

But there's hope. Like I posted before. It only takes 21 days to break a bad habit and 7 days to break a good habit. But the opposite is true too, it takes less than 7 days to start a bad habit and 21 days to start a good habit.

— Emile (*Something to think about*) Fougere

"MOJO"

There have been many songs written about this subject. "I've got my Mojo working," "Mojo Mama," "Mojo Boogie," and more. People write poems about it. The list goes on and on. Why? Because, it's what gets us up in the morning, it's what helps us make it through the day, it's what helps us sleep at night. Without it we have no reason to live. That's why people fall into depression. When I became sick a while back, it almost happened to me. I lost my Mojo, so to speak, I was down in the dumps. I won't go into detail. I thought, what's the point of living? When your sick it's easy to feel this way. So what can you do? You have two choices, 1. Do nothing and get worse or

2. Do something about it. "*Fight.*" That's what I did, I fought. I'm not saying that it's easy for everyone, but it could be. The first thing I did was I started to get busy. I started exercising for my health, then I started eating better, then I started reading for my mental health and then I started thinking better, which led to this (*writing down my thoughts*) and this is good, for me, anyway. If I didn't write them down then they would keep me awake at night and fester, (*not healthy*). You on the other hand, have to find what's good for you, and do it. Another thing that helps is positive thinking, a lot of positive thinking.

Everyone has their ups and downs in life and I've had my fair share. I had my music, which was a good thing for a few years. Then I found Jesus once. That helped for a while, I was married twice (good at first, bad in the end). Now I have Noella, hoping that's permanent. I've had good jobs and I've bad jobs. I've had good luck, I've had bad luck, I've had good cars and bad cars (*never a Gremlin*). It seems, good or bad, nothing lasts forever, except beer & ice cream. Not even sex is forever. Did I say that out loud?

— Emile (*never give up*) Fougere

WHAT TO BELIEVE, WHAT NOT TO BELIEVE – PART TWO

Bullshit makes the grass grow greener *but* it does nothing for the brain or the mind. I just don't know who or what to believe anymore. Do you? If you do, can you tell me and can I believe you? I have heard from lots of people and do you know what? I'm not sure what to believe any more. I know I might get an argument, because everyone is torn. I'm torn too.

I don't know which politician to believe. I don't know which doctor (not witch doctor) to believe. I don't know which scientist to believe. It seems like everyone is lying to us. Teachers, priests, parents, police, friends and relatives. Half the time I can't believe what I say. Everything makes sense and nothing makes sense. Especially when it comes to the virus AND the vaccine. "Cut the CRAP." Please.

Does the word scam mean anything to you? It's just another word for lie. Have you ever been scammed. I have. Believe me. If I had a bigger forehead I would have a big S (*for sucker*) there. Now I have a big C there for Check things out or a big L for learned my lesson. I once bought a plastic box with a blue light in it, it was supposed to attract mosquitoes and kill them, yea right. I killed more mosquitoes with my windshield driving to Moncton and back in the winter. If I was to put food in it the mosquitoes could use it to hibernate in the winter. And then there was the box that could turn your bedroom into an ice box during those hot days in the summer. It couldn't even turn an cardboard box into an icebox. My ceiling fan did a better job of cooling me down.

I don't have a lawn but now I know what I could do with all this bullshit. I could make a fortune. I could be the next Trump or Trudeau. I'd be rolling in it. Money not bullshit. That would be stupid.

— Emile (*Dahhh*) Fougere

PAST, PRESENT AND FUTURE

Have you ever wished you could go back in time and change something in your past? I think about it a lot. And if I did, what would happen to my present? Would everything change like in the movie "butterfly effect?" I think everyone thinks about it once in a while. It's the thing movies are made of. But the thing is, no matter how much we wish and hope that this were true, sorry. Not possible. And it's probably a good thing. All we have is the present. What we do with it is what's important. And what we do with it determines our future. Our future can change in an instant. Not to be morbid, you can die in so many different ways. You can win the lottery, which may be a good thing or a bad thing. Life (*shit*) happens. There are so many things that can determine your future if you think about it. The country you were born in, the color of your skin, the language you speak, how much or how little money your parents have, if you have one parent or two. But the funny thing is in all of these circumstances your future could go in any direction depending on the choices *you* make any time along the way. Another thing that can change your future is the influence that others might have on you, like teachers, coaches and friends etc... All in all, I think I've had a pretty good life.

Sometimes I still wish I could go back and change a few things, like not smoking, or eating too much sugar or bought that mosquito trap . My bad. I don't regret all the beer I drank. That's life and you have to live with it, good or bad.

— Emile (*Back to the future*) Fougere

ALLERGIES, SIDE EFFECTS & POISONS

Do you know how many different kinds of allergies there are in the world? The number is staggering. Some people have a few, some have a lot and some have none. Why is that? No one knows. Some of these allergies are mild (*just rashes*) and some have been known to kill. There are many different forms these allergies might take. I'm not an expert so I don't know. If one thousand people die from eating peanuts, does that mean we should protest or take peanuts of the shelves. No, what they do is make a vaccine for people who are allergic to peanuts. That makes more sense.

Did you know that when you take drugs or are given vaccines you can be affected in the same ways? Who's to say that you are not allergic to medications or vaccines? I have heard of many different kinds of reactions to the corona virus vaccine. Examples: sore arms, rashes, temporary paralysis, your keys sticking to your body. Myself, I suffer from tremors and I need to take medication for this, and without my medication I can be in a lot of pain and so after I took the vaccine my medication was rendered useless for two weeks. I was not sure if this was permanent (*panic time*) or not, but it wasn't, thank God. Just a side effect, one in a million.

That's the thing, we don't know. Like the flu vaccine shot, should we get it? I don't know. People do die from the flu. Maybe not to the extent of the corona virus or peanuts but still.

Did you know that poisons are a lot like allergies and vaccines, they also can give you a bad reaction or they can kill you. Some poison, in the right quantity have been known to cure people.

It wasn't that long ago that doctors use to bleed you to make you better or use leaches to cure you. Now if you take a vaccine your condemned and if you refuse a vaccine your condemned. Should a person be condemned for not taking a flu vaccine or any kind of vaccine or medical treatment that doesn't go along with what is considered normal? And who is to decide what is normal? Everybody should be able to decide for themselves and no one should be able to tell you differently. I know I said that out loud.

— Emile (*I know I'm not normal*) Fougere

A TALE OF TWO SHITTIES

"It was the best of times, it was the worst of times." Sound familiar? It was required reading when I was in high school. Like Hamlet and Tom Sawyer. I never did understand Hamlet even when the teacher explained it. Not even after I seen the movie. No more Shakespeare for me. I was more a Tom Sawyer and Tom Swift fan. Anyway, I digress. My point is, some say we , right now, are living in the worst of times but are we really? I met a man years ago, before all this, who told me he had traveled all over the world and had seen many beautiful sights but all in all he said the best place to live in was Canada.

I know things have been bad since the Corona Vitus started, for everyone and it seems like there hasn't been too much cooperation in the world. I'm sure the government is doing what they feel is right , making rules to protect us. E.I... Masks, social distancing, shutting borders which has led to job losses and closed businesses. I hope this was not their intention. They did try to make thing better by helping people and businesses that were affected. The problem is you can't please everyone. In retrospect they made a few blunders along the way like opening the borders too early and having an election during the pandemic, just to name a couple.

But I won't nit pic. But they did give us free Covid tests and free vaccines. Thats something you won't get in some countries.

On the other side of the coin is tails (just kidding). On the other side of the coin, to be fair. It's nice that we do live in a free country, *but*, you knew I was going to say *but*, sorry, to those who don't agree , *but*, are all these protests really necessary? Can't we just agree to disagree and believe me there has been a lot of disagreeing. The only thing missing is a capital insurrection. Wait for it. I hope it doesn't come down to that. That's all Canada needs. We're better than that. Aren't we? When I first wrote this it hadn't happen yet. I'm not going to say it. I'll just bite my tongue. Ouch.

— Emile (*oops*) Fougere

MYSTERIES OF THE MIND

I was reading an article on google the other day having to do with the mind and how it works. In this article it talked about this man who heard voices and I mean voices, not just one voice but two. These two voices would argue and fight with each other ,very loudly, in his head and it almost drove him crazy. He had to go see a psychiatrist. The psychiatrist couldn't get rid of the voices so, he got council for the two voices in his head and now they get along and they don't fight anymore, peace at last. I hear voices in my head too but thats just me thinking. Don't be alarmed, everybody does it. If you don't your not normal unless you answer back.

Back to mysteries of the mind. Hearing things is not the only mystery of the mind. I have my own mystery of the mind that you may find strange, to say the least. I hope I'm not the only one. If I am, maybe I should go for help or just enjoy it. Here it is. When I close my eyes I see things, mostly at night.

At first I thought I was dreaming, then I realized I was not asleep. I'll give you some examples of some of the things I would see. You know that commercial first choice hair cutters where they show this head of a person, then his face changes from one face to another to another to another, I've seen something like that before the commercial even came out. Sometimes it was even monster faces. Other times, I would see like a small TV screen at a distance with a TV show on it. I don't know what it was, no sound. One time just before my dad died I saw my father laying down, looking sickly and he looked like he was talking at high speed but there was no sound coming out of his mouth, a short time later he died. Some times I see miles and miles of just gravel roads or miles of brick building, stuff like that. It looks so real, like I could almost touch it. Some things I see I can't even talk about. One night I thought my eyes were open and I thought Noella was facing me with her eyes open so I open my eyes and she was facing the other way. To make sure I wasn't dreaming I closed my eyes and there she was looking at me again. Just the other night I was facing Noella and I saw an old man with a white beard and hair hovering over her. These visions have been happening to me for years, so they don't bother me or scare me any more. You get use to it like tinnitus. You have no choice, you live with it. You would be surprised what you can get use to in life. When I see these things I'm sure my eyes are open and I have to check to make sure. Some of you may think I'm crazy and maybe I am but at least I'm having fun. I can't afford brain surgery so I'll just live with it and Noella will live with me. Did I say that out loud? No, that was just a little voice in my head. Go away! I'm in trouble now I'm talking back. Since all this happened I found out it was all the medication I was taking, so I cut them out. No more hallucinations. Fun while it lasted. I stopped because of the other side effects which were harder to live with.

— Emile (*mind-boggling*) Fougere

I DID IT MY WAY. DID YOU?

I could write out all the words to this Frank Sinatra's song but that would be too easy so I'll just do it my way. Like I've mentioned before in my other posts, I'm 73 years young and getting younger, but not better looking. I took a pole. I've lived a pretty good life. To look at me you might not think so. I've had my ups and downs but I just call the downs life's experiences. Some people would call them hell. Without life's experiences how can you grow. You can't. When you were a baby if you didn't get up every time you fell you would still be crawling today. For some of you who drink to much maybe you still do. Sorry, I couldn't resist it. All the experiences I've had, good or bad has made me the man I am today. I've had different girl friends, different marriages, lots of friends, a few bands I played in, lots of different jobs over the years and one business. I've had hard jobs and easy jobs. Over all I was pretty healthy most of those years, anyway, I can't complain. All the things that we live through in life, good or bad, happy or sad, makes us who we are. I'll give you an example. Did you know how much pain you have to endure to learn how to play a guitar, it's not easy on the fingers. But when you finally can play, what joy. Some people just give up. Sad to say, some people give up when it comes to life too. There were lots of times in my life I wanted to give up. I'm glad I didn't. And, "I did it my way." You can do things my way if you want, but then you won't be you. You would be me and that's not good.

— Emile (*my way or the highway*) Fougere

MEMORIES

<u>This is a long one; don't fall asleep</u>

Yesterday I made a date with some of my family to meet at the Legion for a few drinks. I was at Sobeys at 1:30 when my brother Joe called me and said, " I thought you were coming to the legion". I said, "I thought we would be meeting at 2:00." He said, "No, I said 1:00." I said, "I'll be there as soon as I'm finished here." When I got to the Legion he reminded me that he had told me 1:00 and I told him I didn't remember him saying 1:00. The reason I thought it was 2:00 was the last two times we went it was at 2:00. Anyway to make a short story long, we got into a discussion about it at the Legion and my sister said, "Why don't you write about it on facebook?" so here it is. Speaking of Joe, when he retired and moved back to Shediac, he was in the habit of calling everyone Buddy, probably because he couldn't remember their names but always remembered mine. I must have one of those names that's hard to forget.

Memory is a funny thing, not funny ha ha. Well sometimes it can be funny ha ha. Has it ever happened to you that when you go to the living room to do something and you forget why you went there or you go to put something in the cupboard and you end up putting it in the fridge. Been there done that. That's one kind of forgetting. Another, if you go to the mall and you forget where you parked your car that's one thing but if you forget what a car is that could be something altogether different (Alzheimer's). Someone told me a few times if you keep telling yourself that you have a bad memory you can talk yourself into having Alzheimer's. I don't believe that, otherwise I would have it by now. I read somewhere that there are two parts in your brain, and if they are exercised regularly by reading you can avoid Alzheimer's. Novels can stimulate one part of your brain and educational information stimulates another part of your brain. I forget the name of those two parts of the brain. Go figure. Myself I like mystery novels and medical and scientific information. Maybe I should read books on how to improve your memory. But to each his own. It's your brain.

The thing is, we are all imperfect and our memories will never always work 100%. There are people who can memorize whole books, hundreds of songs, hundreds of names. Noella is one of those people who can remember hundreds of names, me on the other hand not so much. When I started seeing Noella it took me a month to remember her name. One night I was singing karaoke and I said I'd like to dedicate this song to ahhhh, my girl friend, I drew a blank. Some days I still have trouble remembering my grand children's names. There are just certain names I have trouble with. They should have consulted with me before naming them (*just kidding*) maybe. Even my parents should have consulted with me before naming me. Seriously my name is Emile not Emily.

I basically have to write almost everything down.Even these thoughts, if I don't write them down when I think of them they disappear in no time, never to be heard of again. I have to write down when I take my insulin and my medication, if I don't, I'll either forget to take them or forget if I took them. I don't have to do that when it comes to eating, exercising or reading, I don't forget everything. I'm not that bad yet. Am I? Maybe, Noella would disagree with me. Is my head still on?

— Emile ?????

HEALTH

I think about my health a lot. Do you? I try to read about what's healthy for you and what's not and I'm confused. First they tell you salt is bad for you and sugar is bad for you, then TV dinners, then processed foods, meat that is fed certain foods, fish that come from the ocean with too much mercury. You can't eat fruits or vegetables because they are sprayed with pesticides, caned foods are not good for you, food wrapped in plastics are poison. Have I left anything out? Probably, Im not an expert. My only option , if I was rich, is to buy a farm in the middle of nowhere and grow and raise my own food. But, even then what are my chances? I would still have to deal with pollution and the ozone layer and lead poisoning is everywhere. I might be healthier but for how long?

Another thing I was wondering. All these experts that write all these wonderful books on what to eat what not to eat, which, by the way, seem to contradict each other like the doctors and scientists who talk about Corona Virus. What do they eat? Are they diligent at what they write about? Are they healthy? I don't know, probably not.. Me, I eat what I have to, to survive. It might kill me some day, maybe not. I don't think so. I take everything I've read with a grain of salt (not literally) just a pun. I exercise moderately, I'm careful what I eat, (not too much junk food or take out) I don't over eat, I don't drink too much alcohol and I don't smoke. Another thing that is not mentioned enough in books is to avoid negative or toxic people.

Only started making most of these changes when I was 70 and I was already sick. So now I am feeling 100% better because of all these changes. I don't know if I'll live to be 100 but you never know but I'll just take it one year at a time. Wish me luck. Maybe I should start smoking pot. Hmmmm. What do you think? Just a THOUGHT.

— Emile (*in moderation*) Fougere

.

RETIREMENT

Well, I've been retired for a while now. So far so good. I love it
????????? I keep myself pretty busy despite Corona Virus. There's
only one problem. (Only one?) I dream about work all the time.
The good news is I don't have to pay taxes, the bad news is I don't
get paid. More bad news, the boss is a real jerk, the good news
I'm self employed. More good news I don't have to worry about
getting a sore back or calluses. I can't fall asleep on the job since
I'm already asleep. I don't understand why some people worry so
much about what their going to do when they retire. Never a dull
moment. "Help." I've heard some people say, "I'm busier now
than I was working." If you are, then you are a workaholic. Sorry.
Me, I'm back to being addicted to watching TV. Just kidding,
maybe.

— Emile (*retiree*) Fougere

THINK POSITIVE

Over the years of reading I have come across many books that talk about positive thinking. The most popular being the Bible. Another, "The power of positive thinking" another "The Secret." Do you know where & when negative & positive thinking begins? It begins sometimes as early as the day we are born or earlier, believe it or not. Some parents try to instill positive thoughts in us early and succeed, for a while, and then TV (cartoons) come into the picture (pun). It's true not everyone is affected by TV but who's to say who? Maybe I was, maybe I wasn't. If I would have been 6ft 2", 180lbs., maybe I would have been the bully instead of the bullied. Who's to say. Then we go to school and a whole new set of negative things come into the picture, negative teachers and negative students.

Let's get back to positive thinking. I think with the right motivation anyone can be positive but you have to work at it and you have to fight against the negative. It's funny how negative thoughts and ideas come so easy and positive thoughts and ideas are dismissed so easily. Like they say, "If good things were easy, where would be the challenge?" Bad is so easy, that's why everyone is doing it. We are living in a world right now in which it is hard to be positive. Believe it or not we are being conditioned *still* to think negative. By the media, by the people around us and sometimes by our own thinking. It's important to question everything we hear and see, even ourselves. Even we can be wrong . Even I can be wrong. I know it's hard for you to believe. One time I though I was wrong and it turned out I was right. See. I hope your not too disappointed.

— Emile (*on the fence*) Fougere

P.S. If you have any thoughts on my thoughts don't be shy.

I can take it. I'm positive. I think.

NON DISCLOSURE AGREEMENT

PLEASE READ: THIS IS IMPORTANT

I was sent an e-mail a while back concerning diabetes . What it said was that diabetics were being fooled into thinking that there is no cure. That there has been a cure for thousands of years and the pharmaceutical companies have known about this for years. This is not the first time I've heard about this. I've heard this spiel at least a half dozen times about different diseases and it sounds like the same voice delivering almost the exact same story. Each time I hear these stories they are trying to discredit big pharma and I don't understand why. I'm not saying they are lying but I don't know if they are telling the truth. It just sound a little fishy. Maybe there's a reason for it, I don't know. This is what I have trouble with. There are millions of doctors and millions of nurses and millions of pharmacists and millions of lab technicians all over the world who have vowed to do no harm but (presumably) have at the same time all signed a non disclosure not to say anything about all these cures for all these diseases. Does that make sense to anyone? If people are willing to lose their jobs over a vaccine , why would so many people do such a thing. If you were one of these millions of people would you break your vow and say nothing so a few thousand people could get rich? Did they take these jobs to make someone else rich or to save lives? If you did I feel sorry for you. I hope I'm wrong. Think about it.

— Emile (*there's nothing funny about this*) Fougere

THE BRAIN

The brain is the most fragile and complicated part of the human body. You might feel differently if you ever stubbed you big toe but you would be wrong. In life, there are so many things that can go wrong with the brain, that's why so many precautions are being taken these days to prevent brain damage. I remember when I was a kid, there was no such thing as hockey helmets or bicycle helmets, which is why I probably need spell check today.

Also, there are so many problems caused by what people do to each other mentally. Child abuse, verbal abuse and physical abuse, War. Then there's bullying, (been there) not my happiest moments. Can't forget sexual abuse (been there too) I don't know too many people who haven't been there, even the abusers, sorry to say. It had to start somewhere. I'm glad I didn't pay it forward. When it comes to any kind of abuse not everyone is affected the same way. Personally, I think I did quite well. I didn't kill anyone or myself. When it comes to the brain anything is possible.

They say everything is a choice but is it, or is it a sickness of the brain. Most people who have a problem no matter how small, think it's their fault and it may not be, so they live their life in fear, not seeking help. Maybe all it was, was a brain aneurism or a brain tumor. There have been so many cases of boxers, hockey players, football players just to mention a few who became violent only to find out that they had brain tumors, go figure. I mentioned in one of my other posts that I see things when I close my eyes at night and sometimes even with my eyes open. Since I got sick two years ago things have not been the same. I went for an MRI and the DR said I was normal. That's good. But what's normal anymore? The world is not normal anymore. I think if you look in the dictionary the definition of normal has changed. That's odd. Usually I try to throw in a little levity in my thoughts but there is nothing funny about mental illness.

— Emile (*normal, maybe*) Fougere

ESSENTIAL TREMORS

I don't know how doctors came up with that name but it was not apropos. Because there is nothing essential about this sickness. I'm not 100% sure but I think I've had it since I was a kid. I use to shake a lot around pretty girls and bullies. Maybe that's a different problem. I tremble more when I become stressed.

I have to tell you this funny story. I can tell this story because I can relate.. This guy had tremors and he was at the bank standing in front of the teller with his hands in front of him and he was shaking it looked like he was masturbating but he wasn't. Ever since then whenever I go somewhere I make sure I keep my hands in my pocket. It just looks like pocket pool.

When I started playing drums it came in pretty handy for drum rolls. When I got older I had to start sitting down to pee, because it got pretty messy and it would rust the baseboard heaters. I had to stop going to the barber because my head wouldn't stop shaking long enough for him to cut my hair let alone trim my moustache. That's why I shave my head now., with an electric razor, otherwise it could be dangerous. It's a good thing we don't have to use straight razors anymore. My mother passed diabetes to me and I passed tremors to my kids. We are such a giving family. Who knew? There are a lot of things I could mention but I won't, you might not see the humor in it. You have to find humor in your life or you will be crying all the time and we don't want that. Watching me type is funny too funny to others but frustrating to me.. Just to mention a few. I could tell you more but it might be easier for me to go on Canada's Got Talent as a comedy routine . Remember this, there are people worst off than you and me. I'm just glad I wasn't born worse off. I could have been.

— Emile (*Shake, rattle and roll*) Fougere

15 MINUTES OF FAME

Believe it or not, from the time we are able to accomplish anything we want our 15 minutes of fame. "Look at me Mommy," "Look what I can do." And it doesn't stop there. When we get older, it doesn't stop especially with boys. We try to get the attention of that special girl. Think about it, why do guys join sports, or girls become cheer leaders? I could be wrong, deep down inside, but most people have an ulterior motive for (*some or most*) of the things they do. I am probably just as guilty as the next person, ok I am.

I'm no saint. Speaking of saints, I don't know if Mother Teresa was ever canonized a saint, I don't think so. There was already a saint Teresa. Did you know that St. Teresa is the patron saint of headaches, look it up. I wonder who the patron saint of hemorrhoids is?

Another famous person in history who got his 15 minutes of fame is the man who invented the toilet. His name was John Crapper. Can you see why he changed it the toilet? It was either The John, The Crapper or The Toilet. What would you have picked? I'm sure his relatives had a big say in his decision. I'm sure he wished he had a choice in being named, John Crapper.

I have had a few 15 minutes of fame in my life, if you want to call them that. I played drums in a few bands to impress girls and it worked. I sang in bands to impress people and I sang karaoke to impress people. According to some people that is not much of an accomplishment. I was a stripper (floor stripper) to be more specific. I wasn't trying to impress anyone, well maybe my clients. You know how I hate to talk about myself, so enough about me.

Everyone has their own way of getting their 15 minutes of fame. Some good and some not so good. Take Donald Trump pleeeeeese. I don't think it was his intention to become known as an infamous lier, but look at him now. Rosa Parks became famous and all she had to do was sit down. Yet there are people out there that do things and don't even care if they are recognized for what they do. They may not even get 15 minutes. Do you know what they are called? They are called HEROES.

— Emile (*only famous for 15 minutes*) Fougere

CONSPIRACY THEORIES

Definition: A conspiracy theory is an explanation for events or situation that invokes a conspiracy by sinister and powerful groups, often political in motivation, when other explanations are not probable.

This may not always be the case. It can start as small in some cases, like a rumor, a lie or gossip. It's amazing how little things can escalate into, well almost anything, even war. Families have stopped speaking to each other over small things like rumors or gossip. Towns have been divided because of lies and racial differences.

Imagine a town or a country being divided because we don't or can't agree. Some people tease me because I drink bud light, should I punch them in the face? Some people pick on me for being a Detroit Red Wing fan, ok they maybe justified there, big deal. I'm also a sci-fi freak. Do you want to beat me up for that too? Boy do I have a lot going against me. I better stop while I'm ahead or behind. Enough about my good qualities.

Back to my point. Conspiracies. There are so many, where to start. UFO's? Been there done that. Religion Nahhhh, too controversial for me. Did you know there are still people who still believe the world is flat and that men didn't really go to the moon. Corona Virus, now theres a possibility for a family divider. I can see that starting to divide countries. People are starting to protest already and you know what that can lead to. I'm going to stop there. There's a new conspiracy, someone started on facebook, if you can believe it, that snow tires are just something someone started to make money and that someone is producing snow and putting on the ground at night so we have to buy snow tires and maybe even shovels, heaven forbid, damn you Canadian Tire. Talk about a scam. And I fell for it. Fool me once shame on you, fool me twice shame on me, stop fooling me.I hope you didn't believe that. Gotcha.

— Emile (*sucker*) Fougere

THE ETHER

I don't know if you have ever heard of this before. I read about this many years ago and I was thinking about it a few days ago and I thought I should write about it. The ether comes in many forms. What it is, is the ability to hear things with your mind from different sources. I'll give you examples. Moses was inspired by God to write the Old Testament and the Apostle Paul was inspired to write the New Testament from God. The scientist and inventor Tesla was presumed to have been given his knowledge by way of *the ether* from *Aliens*. Now the book says *the ether* can come from different sources. They're like radio waves, you can't see them. They can come from space, they can come from radio broadcasts, they can come from someone else's mind. I'll give you an example, (maybe just a coincidence) I was singing a song one day and I happened to turn on the radio and that same song was playing at the same spot where I was in the song, dou, dou, dou, dou. Anyway.

All these THOUGHTS that I write about I'm not sure where they come from. I wake up during the night and I can't sleep and I just start thinking and if I don't get up and start typing, those thoughts will disappear like dreams. Sometimes they even come to me even during the day like this one. I'm not saying my thoughts are inspired by God or aliens, dou, dou, dou, dou,. Maybe I probed your mind while **you** were sleeping, keep one eye open.

— Emile (*The Alien*) Fougere

COMMERCIALS

I have written a couple of times on this subject and I have gotten a few comments back agreeing with me and I thank you. Here is what I wrote just to refresh every ones memory.

Here is what's on my mind. Has any body noticed on some of these sights when your watching something you really like and they throw in a commercial and it's twice as loud as what your watching. I don't know about you, but I'm already hard of hearing and I find it too loud. If I was a cat I would probably hit the roof. I think I know why they do that. I'm talking about the commercials not the cat. So they can sell more of those hearing aids that they advertise on facebook. Am I right or am I right?

This is one of the responses I got:

Most commercials are created to be loud simply so you can hear the advertisement and get your attention. (Mission Accomplished) The Federal Communications Commission (FCC) does not regulate the volume of commercials, nor does it regulate the volume of programs. If the TV has Steady Sound volume control, set it to On.

Does this make any sense to anybody? I hate commercials to begin with, always did. That's why I started watching everything on my computer and when I do watch TV I record what I want to watch so I can fast forward through the commercials, that's just me. And now, what have they started doing on the computer (old movies) they stared putting commercials in old movies on my computer (the same 5 commercials) and the worst part is you can't fast forward through them. The good part is there not too loud, (maybe I should shut up). If you have any comment please let me know and please whisper. Thank you.

— Emile's (*commercial free thoughts*) Fougere

WHAT IS TRUTH?

Its hard to know what truth is any more. It changes from one day to the next, from one person to the next. My truth may not be your truth. What you believe may not be what I believe. Is it butter is it not butter? Is salt good for you or not? Who knows? When I tell people that I'm diabetic they say, "You can't be your not over weight." That's what they believe. They say money can't buy happiness, but it can keep away poverty.

When I was young there was a movie entitled, "If you don't stop it you'll go blind." You know what *it* refers to. Is *it* true or not. The next movie after that was, "I'll just do it till I need glasses." If *it* were true 99.9% of all men in the world (according to statistics) would be blind or would at least need strong glasses. If that were true then optometrists and people who make glasses would be richer than plumbers. Another thing, that would mean an end to wars. Nobody would be able to aim a rifle. Just saying. Touchy subject?

— Emile (*not blind yet, but I do wear glasses*) Fougere

FOR SENIORS

Young people can read this too.

You don't have to if you don't want to. Do I have your attention? This is not a mini thought. If you are over 65 and you want to live to be 100 and healthy you will want to read this. Two years ago I thought I was on the verge of being put into a senior home. I was only 70. I had trouble walking around, I had trouble standing once I sat down. I had to sit down to take a shower. I would fall down a lot. I lost 30 pounds. What to do? What to do?

The first thing I did was I started to eat better, then I started to exercise. Then I started taking multi-vitamins. All this seemed to help. I started gaining weight, I stopped falling down, I got stronger. I started to feel better.

Just lately I read a book on how to live longer and healthier by just doing a few more thing in my life. It seems I was already on the right path. And it's not all that hard. Here are some of the things we can do.

Eat less (no junk food) this way you save money 20%

Exercise at least 30 minutes/day, a tread-mill would be good for your heart., and you can get one on kijiji hardly used for next to nothing. When I started on the tread-mill in July I could barely walk 3 minutes, now I walk 15 minutes and run two minutes. Not bad for a 73 year old with a bad heart.

Turning down your heat in the winter can help you live longer too and you can save money on your electric bill.

Another thing that is good for prolonging life is resveratol which is found in red wine (Pinot Noir). Drinking this wine can add an extra 5 years or more to your life. (In moderation).

This is a quote from Dr. David A. Sinclair, PhD:

Lifespan. Why we age - and Why we don't have to.

I felt better just reading the book. It gave me hope. It made me feel like I was on the right track. If you need any pointers or encouragement you can find me on facebook. This will help you feel better and live longer but it won't make you better looking my girlfriend will attest to that except at night when she takes her glasses off.

On a side note I feel that science and doctors are taking three steps forward and politicians and greedy people are bringing us two steps back and that is why we can't live as long as we should be able to. Something to think about. I know only people who like to read will read this. Pity.

— Emile (*Live long & prosper*) Fougere

DREAMS

When I talk about dreams I am talking about two different kinds of dreams. . One is the kind in which we have nocturnally when we sleep, the other is the kind we have about life.

I've been told some people don't dream. Sorry to hear that. I like dreams, most of the time. Their like Oculus you don't have to pay for. The funny thing about dreams is that sometimes you could be asleep for 15 minutes and have a dream and it could feel like you were dreaming for a whole day or two or the opposite, you could be asleep for eight hours and it felt like twenty minutes. Now that is weird. Sometimes your dreams can feel so real it could feel like your in the matrix. Let me know what you think. I would like to write a book called WEIRD DREAMS and I would like you the people to send in your weird dreams to me and I would put them in my book. Now that would be cool. What do you think? Best seller, Right? Since I wrote this I already have over forty pages of Weird Dreams from people.

Now, the other kind of dream. What do you want to be when you grow up? kind of dream. A fireman? A baseball player? A rockstar? It's funny nobody's ever said jockey, or lawyer or politician or clown (well maybe a clown). I became a mechanical draftsman because it was the only course that was open at the time. At one time I was drawn to the arts , just not drafting. Music and painting,yes. It was never my dream to be a writer let alone a reader (just a hobby) but here I am. I can't even type. Go figure.

— Emile (*one finge*r) Fougere (*I have more than one finger*)
Really I do..

DAMNED IF YOU DO AND DAMNED IF YOU DON'T

I don't know how many people are going to read this but I hope it's a lot. If you like it and you agree with it pass it on to as many people as you can. Because this situation that is going on in Canada and the US is going to affect a lot more people than you may realize in many more ways than you may realize. It's a no win situation, believe me. I'm not a genius and I can see when its all over the trucking companies will not lose much but the truckers will, the cost of all products will double but wages and pensions will not. The economy will go to hell. Trudeau will lose his job but it won't matter because he will still have his mansion on the hill and his cottage in the country and his large pension to live on. I've noticed that it's the people with the biggest mouths that complain the loudest but it's the quietest that suffer the most. I'm tired of being quiet.

As far as Covid is concerned that's a no win situation too. There are going to be losers on both sides there too, especially where friends and family are divided and that's a pity. Sure there are people having side effects from the vaccines, I was one of them, there were people who didn't die from taking the vaccine, I was one of them, I'd like to think. Why, because, I have a bad heart, strike one and I'm diabetic, strike two. I was torn. Should I take the vaccine or not. It was a tough decision. I listened to both sides. Damned if you do and damned if you don't. I thought, better safe than sorry. I thought. What doesn't kill you..... well you know the rest. If you were in my place what would you have done. Something to think about. Flip a coin?

I'll give you a few example of a few things that were forced upon us in the past and you tell me if you regret these things being imposed upon you. Seat belts, child restrains, drinking & diving laws, child abuse laws, spousal abuse laws and the list go's on and on. Would you have protested? Some people resisted. Especially the seat belt law.

When we have children we make rules for them to follow. Should we abandon those rules and let them do what they want. Give them a pair of scissors and let them run around the house. Leave a gun just laying around the house. That's why we elect governments, to stop stupid people from doing stupid things. It doesn't work 100% of the time but it works better than if it was run by just stupid people. So don't elect me.

— Emile (*Seriously, don't elect me*) Fougere

"THE TIMES THEY ARE A CHANGING"

It was true back then and it's still true now. I won't get into the history of it because that would take too much time and I know how much some of you hate to read, so I won't. When it comes to cigarettes, when they first came out they were banned by churches and the governments. Later when the governments seen that there was money to be made, it was a different story. Where were the "convoys" then?

Later, when liquor became a big thing, religions and governments protested, but when the governments seen that there was money to be made from this, stores sprung up all over the world. Where were the "convoys" then?

Again, when drugs started popping up everywhere and the government seen the potential there, then the dollar signs just popped in their eye balls. Then cannabis stores just magically appeared everywhere. What a fiasco that was. But the government didn't give up, after all, it wasn't their money. Anyway that's not the point. Where were the "convoys" then?

The next big thing. Human trafficking. I'm sure there must be a lot of money to be made in that industry. I don't know if Trudeau has checked into it yet. Some country's are already into it and it should't be long before we follow suit. Just saying.

It's funny (*not ha ha*) the things we'll complain about and the things we don't complain about. Like seat belt laws, picking up dog poop laws, wearing masks law, walking six feet apart law, washing your hands law , I won't mention the obvious, etc, etc......

The ten commandments were written for a purpose and people are still fighting them and they are still reaping the consequences.

I could make this thought as long as the "Convoy" but I won't. You're welcome.

— Emile (*breaker, breaker, good buddy*) Fougere

RETHINKING MY CHOICES & TRUE LIES

I saw a few videos and I read some testimonies on line a while back that through me for a loop. I don't want to ruffle anybody's feathers, but it sure ruffled mine. What I saw and read sounded like something out of an Orson Welles film. I couldn't believe it. I know there are bad people in the world but I find it hard to believe that so many people could conspire to hurt so many people world wide just for the sake of money and power. I know mafias do it and criminals do it, but doctors and scientists and politicians? Ok, I can see politicians doing it. Maybe.

At the beginning I wasn't sure about this covid thing but when the media started reporting all these deaths, I started worrying because of my heart condition and my diabetes. They said I was at risk. Again, media hype. I should have done my homework, but I didn't. I just listened to the media like everyone else. I still don't know if the corona virus was real or not but I know more today than I did back then and I'm more scared today than I was back then but, I wanted to know the truth.

I'd like to tell you a true story about a small town , I forget where it was. It was in a small country. It was sheltered from the rest of the country. No communication, no radios, no newspapers, nothing. All around them people were dying from an epidemic. The more that people heard about the epidemic the faster it spread. It spread fast like gossip. So it was mainly because of the media that the epidemic spread so widely but not in this small town and it's the same with this virus.

Another thing that the media can be compared to is Voodoo, believe it or not. If you believe something strong enough it will happen. I've heard of people dying because of Voodoo, if someone put a spell on you. I don't believe it but some people believe it. But the media has that kind of power over people. It's like a super power. They can use it to do good or they can use it to do bad.

What is truth? When it comes to science, one thing can be true one day and the next day it changes according to new findings. It happens all the time. Remember people use to believe the world was flat and believe it or not some still do. When it comes to medicine, one thing is true one day and in the blink of an eye that can change One kind of procedure can kill you and the next thing you know that same procedure will save you. One time they use to suck blood out of you to save your life, next thing you know they are putting blood into you to save your life. Make up my mind. Doctors are not Gods. They don't know everything, and they never will. Did you know at one time you could be fired from your job if you had diabetes? Now they fire you if you don't get a vaccine. Sound familiar?

I don't know which way you are leaning. I had been leaning towards corona virus being real for two years and now I'm not sure. I've heard a lot of people saying that these vaccines are bad for you. Did you know that every vaccine given in the past had side effects too? It's just that back then we didn't have the kind of media that we have today to report it. Lots of people got sick then too, lots of people died too, but many more were saved. It's pretty hard for you to know which way I'm going with this. Like I said before I'm confused too.

When I'm finished this post I'm going to show you what I've found on line. Let me know what you think and give me the proof that you have and I'll weigh both sides and come to my own conclusions. The big problem is who do I believe? Can I believe what you say? Do I believe what they say? What a conundrum. I like that word. Conundrum. Probably because I like drums. I don't know about you but I have been taking different medications for different conditions for quite some time and when they fill my prescription , they give me a one page list of all the side effects of each medication. The list is usually long and scary. (Diarrhea, constipation, not at the same time I hope) Should I refuse to take the medication or should I trust my doctor? He might be out to kill me. There might be a bounty on old people. You never know. That's one less person they have to pay social security too. Oh. Oh. I better not give them any ideas.

— Emile (*baffled*) Fougere

Look up information on Reiner Fuellmich & the court case against him with the government of Canada – You figure out who is lying.

HAIR TODAY NOT GONE TOMORROW

It's funny the things that go through your mind when your trying to sleep and the thing that went through my mind last night was, you wouldn't believe it, **hair.** Right, _hair_. Yes, I am strange. Anyway, back to my story. A theory not fact. Do you know the reason why men have hair on their back and chest? Never crossed your mind right, until now. Because I brought it up.

Here it is, when the hair falls off your head and face they reattach themselves back either to your back or to your chest because, you guessed it, well maybe you didn't guess it, hair is alive. If you have a beard and the balder you are, the more hair you have on your chest and back. Sorry ladies. Unless your into hairy kind of guys.

Another fun fact, I bet you did not know that your hair lives on long after you die. In some cases (bald guys) its the other way around. If you don't want hair on your chest and back start shaving your face and head while your young.

Do you know why most women don't have hair on their back and chest? Another fun fact, most women have long hair so when their hair falls it's too long to stick to their back or chest so then it doesn't have time to grow. I'm not too sure about women with short hair or beards. Make sense? Just a theory. I did go out with a girl who had two hairs on her chest. Just saying. No names. Don't ask.

Anyway. I have nothing against Indigenous people, as a matter of fact I was told I may be part Indigenous, I like that word, Indigenous, Indigenous. The reason I bring this up is because Indigenous people usually have long hair and no beards or use too anyway. Because of this they don't have hair on their back and chest either. Correct me if I'm wrong Chief. Another thing that could prove me wrong is big foot. He's not bald and he has hair on his back and chest, as a matter of fact he has hair everywhere. Just saying.

Something I learned as a carpet and furniture cleaner that proves that hair is alive. I learned this at my brothers house. My sister-in-law is a blond. My other sister-in-law. This is not a blond joke. She has long blond hair and they had a dark couch and chair. While I was cleaning them (the couch and chair), don't get the wrong idea, I noticed that there were blond hairs sticking out of the couch and I pulled them out (the blond hairs) stay with me. It seemed that they had worked their way into the couch as if they were alive, all kinds of them. The hairs were a foot long but they were only sticking out an inch or so. I took the cover off of the cushion and it was just full of blond hairs. I don't know if they all came from her head or they were reproducing. Doo,doo,doo,doo.

I think I could write a book on the subject but I won't. Aren't you glad? Please answer yes so I know your still out there.

— Emile (*Started shaving too late*) Fougere

BUTTERFLY EFFECT

I know I've mentioned this before but this is for a different reason so bare with me. I became sick to the point that I had to stop working, well it was time anyway I was 70, well over my prime. Over my expiry date. To the point I was so sick I was in bed a lot, I had other people doing all my work for me, so it was not worth having a business and it didn't look like I would get any better, so I sold the business. It got so bad I thought I would end up in a home. The last thing I wanted was to end up in a home. I was too young. My pride got the better of me. I thought there must be another way.

Hence the title BUTTERFLY EFFECT.

Have you ever seen the movie Butterfly Effect? It's about a guy who can go into the future sees what has happened and he goes back and changes what he did to prevent what happened and every time he does he changes his future. It either gets better or it gets worse. Now, I'm not saying our lives are like that but our lives are a bit like that. We can see into the future whenever we see someone else's life unfold before our eyes and we can learn from it. Why make your own mistakes when you can learn from someone else's mistakes. It's cheaper that way. That's why we read

EMILE FOUGERE

books to learn how not to make mistakes. That's how I got better, when I was sick, I read up on it. If your sick, your sick for a reason. When I have health problems it turns out I'm having side effects from my medications.

Side Note: One of the side effects of my tremors medications for tremors is tremors. Its like saying that one of the side effects of the medication for diarrhea is diarrhea, not true but ironic if it was true but in my case it is true not the diarrhea but the tremors. Anyway, I digress. My point is all medications have side effects. I've come to learn by reading and learning more, that most of these side effect can be fixed by self acupressure, self reflexology, self massage therapy and other things I've yet to try and there are no side effects. Self acupuncture is a little trickier and more expensive if someone else does it for you so I don't think I'll try it.

We all make choices in our lives that predicts the outcome in the end and we never know. We don't have crystal balls. All we can do is hope for the best and do things in our lives that can help along the way. Like, eat healthier, stop smoking, don't lose your temper, exercise more, love more, hate less.

I know I don't follow the Bible as much as I used to but it doesn't mean I don't believe in it. As a matter of fact it helped make me the man I am today. There is a lot of good in most of the books I have read and I'll keep reading as long as I am alive. You would not believe how many times I reread and have rewritten these thoughts before I sent them out. Because of my tremors and my medication it can be frustrating but it's fun anyway. It gives me something to do in my young age. Like they say if your going to do things right. How does the rest go? Damn medication. I'll quit while I'm ahead. Am I ahead?

— Emile (*Hanging in there*) Fougere

NOTHING TO SNEEZE AT

I wish I had videos of these but it's not possible since all of these can only happen completely by surprise. At this point you have no idea what the hell I'm talking about. Don't despair, there is a method to my madness. I suppose you could plan them but they wouldn't be as funny or spontaneous, if you know what I mean. Some of these are pretty funny and some are pretty gross, so get your puke bags ready.. Now don't get ahead of me.

1. I'm sitting with this cute girl at the top of these concrete stairs and I said something that made her laugh so hard it made her pee and when she does, she starts to slide down the stairs, talk about a slippery slope. The rest is all down hill from there. I tried not to laugh. Really.

2. Have you ever been eating in a restaurant at a table full important people and without warning you sneeze, need I say more. A picture is worth a thousand words and you don't want that picture. These days with all these cell phones you probably would have a thousand pictures.

3. Imagine this. You're brushing your teeth, you mouth is full of tooth past and without warning you sneeze and your mouth explodes, you only have enough time to

take your toothbrush out of your mouth. Tooth past everywhere. All over the mirror, the sink, the faucet. If you were an artist and it would be a paint you could get rich with. But who puts paint in their mouth, these days you never know, not me. Not for love or money. Well maybe money. Someone told me this and I won't say who but when she sneezed she hit her head on the sink, don't worry she didn't break the sink.

4. Here's my top three. Get your bags out.You have diarrhea, ok not you, your on the toilet and all of a sudden you guessed it, you sneeze without warning. Have you ever seen two explosions at the same time from both ends. This is the time you need a camera. Fireworks. Kind of. You had to be there. If you were you must be kinky.

5. It's two o'clock in the morning your fast asleep you have diarrhea and your spooning with your wife and not in a good way if you know what I mean and all of a sudden you sneeze. I'll tell you something, if your looking to find a new way to get into the dog house that's it. This has never happened to me but I know of someone. I still laugh when I think about it. No names. He would kill me.

6. Last but not least. I hope you didn't jump ahead. And if you filled your puke bag grab another. Another diarrhea story. Have you had your Colonoscopy yet. If you know anything about Colonoscopies, if not check it out Anyway, if you have you'll love this. It's a hoot. Not for the doctor in this case, but I'm sure the nurses would have

a good laugh. The patient is laying on the table being prepped for the procedure and is not totally out and the doctor bends over to insert the camera and the patient sneezes and now you know the rest of the story.

— Emile (*I thought I farted but I shit*) Fougere

BUTTERFLY EFFECT (part 2)

I'm on a quest. I've been doing a lot of researching on this subject and I've come to a few conclusions . Hear me out, please. They say when a butterfly flaps it's wings hear in Canada the effect can be felt on the other side of the world. I don't know if this is true or just a metaphor. But, I do know this, that if a negative or positive thought is thought or uttered it can be felt all over the world. Point in fact, the Corona virus. I can't give you an example of a positive thought, because those are few and far between, but they do exist. Positive thoughts rarely make the media.

Negative thoughts and words can be very toxic. They can affect your health, your relationships, your happiness, your prosperity. It can cause health problems, divorce, poverty and even wars. The good news is that positive thoughts can have the same effect. Imagine what kind of world we would be living in if everyone would think positive thoughts. Like I mentioned in thought #24, it's a lot easier to think negative. The reason is that we have been conditioned since the day we were old enough to think to be negative. Imagine what kind of world this would be if positive thinking were taught in school. The possibilities are endless'

When I was sick two years ago, the first thing I did to change my situation was to start thinking positive, I started exercising and I made a few more changes in my life. I think the thing that made the biggest difference was positive thinking. Lately I have been expanding my positive thinking to other areas of my life. It's a hard road but my thinking is getting better. I've lowered my negative thinking to 30% and I've increased my positive thinking by 60% by doing positive affirmations every day. The more affirmations you make everyday the harder it is for negative thoughts to enter your mind. I still have a long way to go. If I can just reach two people and they can reach just two people and so on and so on, I guarantee that in a very short time this world will be a better place to live in. Don't take my word for it, do you own research, you will be amazed like I was. Look up Louise Hay, Dr. Joe Dispensa, Jose Silva and Rhonda Byrnes and many more on YouTube. If positive thinking can help me it can help you. But the secret is to weed out negative thinking. One does not work without the other.

— Emile (*thinking positive*) Fougere

ACCORDING TO HOYLE

Definition: According to plan or rules.

This thought is not directed at anyone in particular but what I'm about to say can apply to anyone even me and it has. Every game has rules that come with the game when you buy them. But, if you want to know the rules you can go on line for verification. Sometimes, among friends, if they agree to change the rules, which is fine as long as everyone agrees.

Long ago when life was less civilized if you cheated you would probably be shot or hanged, or is it hung. Anyway, now, if you cheated someone would probably just overturn the board or never talk to you again. A lot better than being shot or hung, right? So then let the games begin.

That, having been said, lets move on to the *game of life*. Life can be like a game. "How?" you may ask. Well for one thing life has rules too, (*ten to be exact*) and if you don't play by the rules there are consequences.

Before I continue there's one thing I would like to say. Everyone and I mean everyone has been the victim of a broken rule, some very serious and some not so serious. Weather serious or not , it can be quite devastating and if you let it, it can affect you for the rest of your life or longer. The key words here are *if you let it.* At sometime in your life, someone may have hurt you, on purpose or by accident and may not even realize it and you may be mad for a long time. The problem with that is that anger hurts you more than it hurts the person it's directed at, especially if it stays in your heart and on your mind for a long time. The person your angry at may not even know or care.

There are many negative memories and emotions that we hold near and dear to our hearts for a long time. The problem with holding them near and dear to our hearts is that it's hurting our hearts to the point of death, eventually. Not my opinion but a proven fact. I could give you examples of this to the point of this turning into a book. But I won't, for the sake of people who hate to read. You know who you are. I hope you made it this far.

Have you ever heard the expression, "It's better to have loved and lost than never to have loved at all?" Here's a new one," "It's harder to lose a good friend than to have no friends at all." Don't hate, it's not good for your heart. Just saying. Only twenty more pages to go.

Just kidding, maybe.

Here's another old saying I'm going to change for the sake of this topic. "Fool me once shame on you, fool me twice shame on me." Here it comes, get ready for it. "Hurt me once shame on you, hurt me twice shame on me." Never go past twice. You can use it if you want. "Forgive and forget," I didn't make that one up. That's why it sounds so familiar.

You may not like reading my long thoughts, just remember this. It's a lot harder to write them than it is to read them. It may come from the ether but I'm the one who has to do all the work. When you have tremors it's twice as hard and it takes a lot longer. It's a lot easier with wine.

— Emile (*not so angry anymore*) Fougere

ALL MEN ARE CREATED EQUAL?

Are they really? Only according to the Bible. God made us equal but man changed that pretty quickly.

Football players: 2.7 million/year

Baseball player: 3.9 million/year

Average a-list actor: 45 to 60 million /movie

Average rock star: $100,000 to $1,000,000 per gig

Justin Trudeau: $379.000 not including all fringe benefits which is probably another $40,000.

Ministers in the senate: $160.000./ year plus benefits

I never made even close to that working my ass off.

Doctors: $350,000. / year

Nurses: $90.000./ year

Teacher: $45,000./year. If you're good: $71,000./year

University professor: $156,000./ year

Why does a teacher make less than a university professor? If it wasn't for the teacher there would be no need for the university professor. Shouldn't they both be paid the same? Just a thought.

Police: $97,000 / year

Fireman: $65,000./ year

Factory worker: between $30,000 and $40,000 / year

Health care worker: $45,000./year

Bartenders: between $30,000. and $40,000 /year that probably doesn't include tips.

Bank teller: $40,000. / year

Fish plant worker: $31,200./year

Store clerk: $36,000./year

Waiters & waitresses: between $20,000. & $30,000 / year. I don't know if that includes tips. Probably not.

The average person who works makes $61,000 / year and if he goes on unemployment will receive 55% of his income which works out to $650 / week which works out to $33,800 / year. That sounds about right for middle class but not the average Joe.

Now lets talk about people on welfare. A couple with 2 children: $27,177. A single person with one child: $21,595.

I worked hard all my life for others and for myself. I paid my taxes and I paid into Canada pension and old age pension. What do I have to show for it? Here's the thing, I am barley making ends meet. The cost of living keeps going up and the means to live doesn't. The politicians salaries go up every year and so does his pension if he is retired and he probably still gets all the perks

Senior Citizen: $32,000./ year. Can anybody confirm this? I know I can't. The best I can do is $25,000./ year. Believe me I'm not bragging. I know that there are many who are making less than $20,000./ year. Can't be too good when you see people over 65 working at Sobeys and McDonalds because Canada pension and old age didn't cut it. Who knew? How do you feel about retiring now?

— Emile (*not my statistics*) Fougere

SEEING IN THE DARK

I don't know if it's just me but does anyone else find it hard to watch TV these days? I thought it was hard enough to watch TV in the dark but I find it even harder to watch TV shows and movies that are filmed in the dark. I know I'll be revealing my age here but when I was young we use to get our entertainment on radio, some of you remember that, right? It's TV without pictures. What they would do is act out a show on radio and everything was left to your imagination, like TV for blind people. I asked Seri why they do this and she told me it's because they don't want you to see all the mistakes they make. Really? Or, is it because they save money on their electric bill? That's what I do. If they want to save a lot of money maybe they should go back to broad-casting stories on radio. There use to be a name for that but the name eludes me. If anyone remembers let me know.

If there is anyone out there who is in charge of this , could you please turn up the lighting at least 30% so I can at least see what I'm watching. If it wasn't for the fact that they show the credits at the beginning I wouldn't know who's acting in these show. It's like trying to read a book without my glasses. I've seen a few bad movies out there that should have been filmed in the dark and with no sound. What's next, are they going to film "Wheel of

Fortune" in the dark? I've got an idea, they should film porn in the dark. Just saying. I wrote this thought four months ago and since then I believe they did turn the lighting up a bit with some shows and movies. Thanks for listening.

— Emile (*My two cents worth, five with inflation*) Fougere

I'VE BEEN EVERYWHERE

Have you ever dreamed of traveling the world? Well you can, believe it or not. I've done it and it hasn't cost me a dime. How? You ask. I can tell you in two words, YOU TUBE. That's right, you can go to any country, any town, any village in the world. And the best part is you don't have to worry about things like taking a cab to the airpot, waiting for flights, crowded airports, flight delays or stopovers. They say you can see the great wall of China from space, well I saw it from my living room. I saw the running of the bulls in Spain without getting trampled. I walked through the streets of Calgary without wearing out my shoes. I've been to Tebet. Ive been on the train traveling through Russia and Siberia, (*no war*) and I went to Ukraine and I wasn't boomed and all of the buildings are still there. Another thing you don't have to worry about, getting mugged or run over in traffic. Ladies, you can go to Italy and you don't have to worry about having your butts pinched, unless you like that kind of thing. Me not so much. You can see everything without buying everything, unless you like doing that, in witch case there's always Amazon. Fifty years ago I lived in Zweibrucken ,Germany and I always wondered what it looks like now, so, I went on my computer and I typed, "You Tube, Zweibrucken, Germany." Ta ra, there it was in all it's glory. Just for the fun of it I typed, "You tube, Shediac New Brunswick, the Lobster capital of the world," again ta ra there it was. Shediac is right outside my door and I didn't have to leave my home.

They have these devises (like goggles) and you can buy programs to see the same things in 3D which is better than You Tube. It's like being in a hologram on Star Trek Enterprise. You can go around the world in less than 80 days. OK, you can't try the local cuisine, so just eat a hot dog and pretend it's Italian pizza or just order out a pizza and you don't have to pretend and get some wine while your at it. That was fun, wasn't it? It was good for me, was it good for you?

— Emile (*World traveler*) Fougere

SCAMS

Definition: A dishonest scheme, a fraud.

Scamming people is not new. It's not as old as the "oldest profession in the world," but it's right up there with it. Some religions have been scamming people for thousands of years. You don't have to take my word for it. Look it up. That's an order! Just kidding, but do it. Another scam that comes to mind is people who would ride into town with their wagons, (*Gypsies*), selling magic potions, elixirs, medicine. A rose by any other name is still a rose. To add to the scam they hire some people posing as sick people to add to the drama and *voila* you've been sucked in. Once people are fooled to believe, then placebo kicks in which makes it more believable for others. No harm, no foul. Even in our modern day of medicine we are purposely fooled with placebos. If they work great, if not no harm, no foul. In old days these charlatans would be tared and feathered, now they are called pharmacists, scientists and doctors and given awards.

I haven't even gotten into the big stuff. Internet fraud. Now there's a market worth pursuing if I was a crook. I could be as rich as Trump. I'm glad I got that out of my system.

Here are a few of my experiences, yes, I'm a sucker for punishment, to the point Mastercard told me if I get caught again they would cut me off. I guess that's better than being tarred and feathered. Some of these I have mentioned before but worth repeating.

1. I ordered a small plastic container with blue neon lights, it catches mosquitos and kills them. **NOT.** Makes a great disco light.

2. A small plastic box that turns any room into a freezer. It couldn't even turn a small box into a freezer. Don't throw your air conditioner out.

3. My all time favourite, a watch that can check your glucose levels. That was two years ago and guess what, *there back.* Better advertising same junk. The good news, it tells time.

4. Here's another one that I get on a regular basis. People who hack other peoples facebook accounts and ask you to be their friend. Sound familiar? They tell you that they just received $50,000 and I could too. Now it's up to $250,000 . Free money from the government. Why would the American government want to give me (a Canadian) money? All I have to do is pay UPS for shipping.

5. Speaking of UPS, this is the one that almost got my Mastercard canceled. They e-mailed me saying that they tried to deliver a parcel and I wasn't there to receive it. And for a charge of $2.00 they would bring it by the next day. Since I was expecting a parcel I fell for it. Since

then, at least once a week they keep trying. No more, I'm serious, leave me alone.

"Fool me once shame on you, fool me twice shame on me." Said the idiot (*me*). While I got your attention does any one want to buy ocean front property in Florida.

— Emile (*gotcha*) Fougere

LIVING FOREVER

There are some people that say yes and there are some that say, (*believe it or not*) no. Some say that it's not possible. Some say, why would any one want to? If everybody lived forever wouldn't the world become over crowded eventually? In order to live forever you would have to stop crime, accidents, natural disasters etc... and that isn't going to happen any time soon. Just remember forever is a long time. Do you know how many people commit suicide these days? It's not because they want to live forever. Most people get bored easy. Imagine living 1000 years or more. You would have to be very rich in order to not get bored in that span of time or longer. Even rich people get bored believe it or not. There are some things that last forever, like karaoke, line dancing, cowboy boots and sarcasm. Some things never die.

Now for those of you who believe in God. I'm not saying I don't and I'm not saying I do. I'll leave that to your imagination. Some say when you die everyone will go to heaven or hell and I'm sure there is lots of room in both for everyone. Some say that 144,000 will go to heaven and many will live on a paradise on earth forever. Like I said in part of the first paragraph I don't know how that is going to work out but I'm sure God knows. Probably no karaoke, no line dancing, maybe cowboy boots definitely no sarcasm. Some things do die.

I've read Revelation a few times and so far, all the signs predicting the end of times have all come true, sad to say, but I talked to someone years ago and he told me that Armageddon was months away and that was 16 years ago. So many predictions so many let downs. I've had a good life, I don't know if I want to live forever.

— Emile (*Happy for now*) Fougere

TIME (Back to the future)

Einstein said that time was relative. Mic Jagger sang that time was on his side. Young people say they have plenty of time. Time means different things to different people. To me, at my age, time is a luxury The only way I can say that I have plenty is if I live to be 120 or 150 and I would have to be in good enough shape and have enough money to enjoy that extra time, but one never knows. Three years ago I thought my time was almost up, but I got a reprieve and maybe it could happen again. You never know. Maybe Einstein was right, maybe time is relative, but relative to what? I know what I'm doing now in the present. What about the future? I can tell you that I will still be writing this post in ten minutes unless I need to go to the bathroom in which case that will change my future and after that I will be going to Karaoke at 6 o'clock. When I post this you will see it in the future but yet it will be my past and you will be seeing it in your present. Mind - boggling isn't it? Probably, some of you lost me at Einstein, but that's not relative. Right Joe? Joe gave me the idea for this time post in the past and now it's my present and now your future. Stay with me, will you. That's not relative to this post. Oh oh. I think I lost track of time, that happens a lot to me. I think, I'm in a time loop, oops, there I go again. Not again? Help me Einstein............. Thank you, that was weird. Time for another beer and a short break. See you in the future............. I'm back, that didn't take long. It was long for me ,was it long for you? I'm back from Karaoke and I had fun but that was in the past, let's think about my future or yours. This is fun I could do this all day. It would be my longest post ever, but that's not relative, or is it? We'll never know, will we?

— Emile (*75 years from now*) Fougere

DO WE HAVE A CHOICE?

Like I've mentioned before I do a lot of reading for the health of my brain, my choice. In so doing I've learned a lot about choices. The thing is you won't find any or some of these things in the bible but some of what I am telling you is in the bible. Here is our first choice in life, even before we are born (*not in the bible*) we can chose what we want to be, where we are born, what color we want to be, what language we want to speak. It has been said that we have lived many lives and each time we die we move on to the next life. When ever we die we become, for lack of a better word (*spirits*) and during that time as a spirit , weather long or short we get to decide. Now if you have lived ten, twenty or thirty lives, when you come back you may want to try something new. Imagine the possibilities. In this book they even suggested that some may even want to be born blind, crippled, poor, male, female or even homosexual. This is the reason I am writing on this subject. I read a post by this guy I can't remember his name, I should know it, like my own name. Oh yea, Emile Vautour. I knew it would come to me, and his last name is the same as my partner.

In the bible it says that men should not lie with men. But, and here's a big but (*not to be mistaken with butt*) it has been suggested that gay people were born that way. Now, I read that a gay persons genes are totally different from male and female genes. To me that means they were born that way. I don't know how factual this is but it's something to think about. If you have been reading my THOUGHTS you know I don't take sides, I just present the (*facts*) as I know them. Why would a scientist lie? Unless he is gay and he wants everyone to believe it. Just saying.If I have made choices while a spirit I don't remember making (*this*) choice. What was I thinking? And I've seen some pretty (*ugly people*), what were you thinking? Just joking, maybe, my bad. I better stop before I get in trouble.

— Emile (*just slap me*) Fougere

THE BIG FIVE-O - NOT MARRIAGE

When I said the big five-o it doesn't mean I was married for fifty years, well, maybe all together. What I meant was that this is my 50th THOUGHT. Stick with the program.

"Love and marriage, Love and marriage go together like a horse and carriage." That use to be true, way back when, but not any more. Now it's a different story or should I say stories. Don't get me wrong some marriages do work but now the statistics tell a different story, some pretty gruesome stories. Sometimes I think a marriage license is just a license to physically and mentally abuse. You probably noticed I didn't end that sentence with the word women. Because women can be abusers too. Surprised? Is nagging considered abuse? Some people would say NO. "It's just in fun," they also say, "it was his or her fault, they had it coming." Fun for who? The first song I mentioned was true, now the new song goes like this, "It's hard to kiss the lips at night that chew your ass out all day long." Again, not just for women. That song was written with a woman in mind. With a few modifications it could just as easily apply to a man. Just saying. Don't get mad people. If you don't like it, stop reading. But, I know you won't. We are a curious species and gluttons for punishment, not abuse. Read on.

When the license is there, spouses think they can do whatever they want and their mate can't do anything about it. That use to be true but not so much anymore. Sometimes even religion played a part in excusing the abuser, especially the husband. They use to ask the wife "what did you do to make him mad?" I suppose it's always easier to blame the wife. I heard of one case in which the husband was a cop. Can you guess which side the cops took? If you are an abuser I guarantee you will not agree with me.

If I was to interview people about their stories and write a book on the subject it would be a thick one. Bible size. I don't want to, it would be a very depressing and stressful book to even write let alone read. It would take a very strong person to do that. That's not me. It would be hard to even tell my own story.

— Emile (*That's just me*) Fougere

ALZHEIMER'S

This is a topic that is near and dear to my heart. My father had Alzheimer's and Noella's sister died not of it but because of it.. For the last few years I have been reading books on memory , the brain and Alzheimer's. I'm not a doctor and I'm not a scientist but I am more informed now than I was before. About six months before Corona I believe I was headed in that direction. The signs were all there now that I think of it. And if anyone had told me I don't think I would have listened. My father didn't until it was too late. What I'm about to tell you is just a theory on my part, so you can take it or leave it. For those of you who have someone close to you with Alzheimer's please listen carefully. I read that Alzheimer's can be caused by alcohol. That might be part of the problem but not the whole problem. I think one of the biggest causes might be medications. It's not hereditary. The reason I say this is when I was on medication, that's when I started having side effect, one of which was memory loss. I was on these medications for a long time and when I stopped it took a long time for my brain to start functioning properly again. I'm not 100% yet but getting there. Another good step for helping is, if they can, is to do some reading, nothing negative. Reading can kick start your brain in the right direction. There are a lot of books and plenty of videos on You-Tube that can be very helpful on positive thinking.

I read all kinds of books. Medical books, science books, mystery novels, anything to keep my mind active.

When it comes to visiting a person with Alzheimer's the biggest problem is, "what's the point they won't even know I visited or not even recognize me." That may be true but it's the loving thing to do. When you visit, what do you do and say? That's the part I'm talking about. What do you do and say?

Keep in mind, their brain is still working. How do I know?

The fact that they are still breathing, walking, seeing, hearing, eating and millions of other things, their brain is still working. Trust me, I know. How much different is Alzheimer's from amnesia caused by head trauma? What do doctors and family do? They get together to help him remember. They bring in people they know to help them remember and pictures, videos etc...

I've mentioned before that I live with tremors. That's a brain disorder too and there's a treatment in the works for that, but medication is not the remedy, believe me. The only temporary remedy is alcohol in moderation. Most of the time I just put up with the shaking even though it can be quite embarrassing and frustrating especially when I'm typing. It sure beats the alternative, terrible side effects.

I'm glad my family was there for me, which is why I decided to start to do something for myself, because I probably would have given up.

Back to Alzheimer's. Here is what I think **might** be a solution worth checking into. I believe I had most of the symptoms for Alzheimer's when I decided to change my lifestyle. These are some of the things others can do to help if you are willing to put in the time.

1. Visit them more often, the more often they see you the easier it will be for them to remember you.

2. Have as many people they know visit more often.

3. Bring up as many memories as you can. That will help fire up the old brain synapsis. They may not remember at first but they will.

4. This one is important. Bring pictures and videos. Visuals are important.

5. If you really care, what have you got to lose and you would have made more memories for yourself if nothing else.

6. If you go as a group you will rekindle memories for each other and have fun in the process.

7. Better a visit to the home than to a funeral parlour.

8. If physical therapy can help limbs why not mental therapy for mental problems. You have two choices, prove me right or prove me wrong.

9. My daughter watched a video of a woman who was getting married and she wanted her father to be "present" for her wedding... He had Alzheimer's and couldn't remember even who she was... So because he loved to paint, she put a paintbrush in his hand with some paint and

a canvas and he came right back to life and knew who she was and even why he was there looking at her in her wedding dress... It was amazing!

It's been proven that the music people listened to when they were younger brings back memories. They sometimes even sing along!!

WARNING: If you are on any medications go on line and check out any and all side effects. As a matter of fact when I was prescribed medications I read the paper that the pharmacist gave me and I saw all the possible side affects and I told my self , it won't happen to me. Boy, was I wrong.

Most of these ideas, I thought were mine, kind of. Some of these ideas that I thought I had, had also been written by Dr. Sanjay Gupta in his book, KEEP SHARP.

— Emile (I *do care*) Fougere

HOMELESSNESS AND MORE

Did you know that in 2021 there were close to 8 billion people in the world and there are lots of people that are homeless, sick, depressed and destitute. I can't give you the numbers but there's a lot. If I could tell you I don't think I want to, it would be too depressing, even for me. Someone posted a question on face book a while back, "What would you do if you had a billion dollars?" I replied, "I would try to help as many people as I could." I don't need that much money, nobody does, *nobody*. I read one time that if all the wealth of the world was distributed evenly everybody in the world could be a millionaire. Can you believe that? I do.

This is just a theory, but if all 8 billion people in the world were to donate 1 dollar every month to some world wide charity imagine all the good it would do? You would have to hire at least a thousand people just to count and distribute the money. That's a thousand new jobs. Then you would have to hire people to build shelters for all these homeless people. And once the word gets out about this project then the communities and business would donate more money and time. Then the people who are helped in time, once their lives have been improved, would start to donate and help. A vicious circle, good vicious.

Do you know who these homeless people are? Do you know their story? What is your reaction when you see them? Do you think, 'what a bum." Do you cross the street to avoid them? If your not part of the solution, your part of the problem. Hard truth? Sorry!

Let me tell you who these people are. Veterans who lost limbs in war, suffering from PTSD, unable to fine or keep jobs because of these problems. Women and children from abused homes, people who lost their jobs because of the economy or Corona Virus. The list is endless. Homelessness is not something that should even exist, but it does, all over the world.

On the other end of the scale. Did you know that Putin has half a dozen private jets with gold toilets and tubs in them. Plus half a dozen yachts, and mansions in more than a dozen countries. The only word that comes to mind is, shameful. If you can think of a better word I'm open to suggestions. What do you think of someone who spends billions of dollars to send spaceships to Mars. Did you know that the Canadian government donated billons of dollars for this project. Do you care whats on Mars? I don't. I like Star Trek as much as the next man, as entertainment, not a goal.

Speaking of entertainment, do you know how much money is spent on entertainment compared to education and health care? If I was to guess I'd say about 100 times more. Awards and lavish parties are spent on entertainment but there are no awards given to nurses, health care workers or teachers, just to name a few. I speak my mind and I don't want an award for it. I've had a good life, not a great life. Great is overrated. I don't know if this post is going to make a difference or not, I know, I at least tried. If you can send this out to as many people as possible, you never know. With LOVE and a positive mindset anything is possible.

— Emile (*the ball is in your court*) Fougere

NEGATIVE VS POSITIVE

In a battle for supremacy between negative and positive, which one do you think would win? About four months ago I started reading the book, "The Secret" it's a great book. It has had a great influence on my life and still does. Do you know which book has the most negative words in it? You guessed it, the dictionary. You would be very surprised how negative you and I can be in the span of just one day. I am amazed every day. It happen when we have company, it happens when we go out with friends, it happens when we talk on the phone. Most of all it happens in our own minds, when we think. Are you surprised? I know I was. When I was writing this book I didn't realize how much I was doing it. When I'm typing these thoughts and I struggle to hit the right keys or hit the key once too often thats when my negative thought jump out at me. F##k,s##t the list goes on and on and on, shall I go on. What takes the most time is trying to correct the mistakes. Then more f##k,s##t etc... I only made 30 mistakes in this Thought so far. I'm proud of my self. I'd pat myself on the back but I would probably miss.

There is a good example in the book, "The Secret" that I like. About Mother Theresa. She was once asked if she would attend an anti-war rally. She said, "No, but if you start a peace rally I'll be in the front lines."

— Emile (*more positive than negative*) Fougere

LEGACY

Definition:

1. The amount of money left to someone in a will. Not me.

2. The long lasting impact of particular events, actions, etc. That took place in the past, or of a person's life.

Do you have a legacy? What is your legacy? Is it a good legacy or a bad legacy? Is it a long time legacy or short time legacy? Money can be a long time legacy or a short time legacy depending on how much you leave. Your name can be a long time legacy or a short time legacy and sometimes it doesn't matter if it's good or bad. Even if it's good or bad it does have an expiration date. Examples of long time legacy's: Hitler, Jesus, the Right brothers, madame Curie, Attila the Hun, Pee Wee Herman (just kidding) maybe, Jack the ripper, Donald Trump (definitely). Just a few examples.

Would you like to have a legacy? How do you want to be remembered? How can you be remembered? There are many ways to be remembered, hopefully without killing someone. If you kill one person you might be remembered for a while but if you're a serial killer you (might) be remembered for a long time like Jack the ripper and Ted Bundy, definitely Hitler. There is one thing that helps these names and others to be immortalized, Books. There are different ways anyone can become immortalized, etched in stone so to speak. Here they are in no particular order, music, paintings, books and porn. Did I say that out loud? Even these ways don't come with a guarantee. Like the old saying, "There are no guarantees in life". Except taxes and death and I really hate those last two.

— Emile (*remember me?*) Fougere

MARIJUANA

Dope, pot, grass, weed, Mary Jane, head (that's a new one to me) doobie, bud, ganja, hashish, bhang, reefer, chronic, herb, muggles, mooter, Mary Warner,Indian hay, loco, love weed, bambalacha, mohasky, mu, tea, blue sage. That's a lot of names just for one, for lack of a better word, product. I got all these names off the internet without making an order not that I couldn't.

People affected by cannabis (ohh, another one cannabis) are "high," "stoned," "out of it," "whacked off their face" or "shit faced."

Some people experience feelings of wellbeing, happy, relaxed or sleepy. There's more. Heightened sense of taste, smell, sound and/ or touch. Here are some I can relate too. Quiet, withdrawn, confusion, anxiety, panic attacks, fearfulness and paranoia. Can even cause mental health issues, psychosis, image distortion, loss of personal identity, hallucinations, respiratory infections, impaired memory, learning ability, increased heart rate. Wow! I did not know all this. Did you? And I thought taking medication was bad. To make things worse, doctors are telling us about all the foods that are bad for us. Even sex can have medical consequences. You don't want to see *that* list. Really you don't.

— Emile (*really you don't*) Fougere

TWIN TOWERS OF BABYLON

I just finished watching the documentary on the construction and destruction of the twin towers and I find the whole thing a bit bizarre. Maybe it's just me. The towers were so massive, they had their own zip code. A city within a city so to speak. They even had their own police force. I'm surprised they didn't have their own hospital and ambulances. Right from the beginning they thought terrorists might try to fly a plane into the building, so they made provisions for that. Another thing I found strange is that they hired a mafia boss (who had his own construction company) to work on the buildings. Because he had the lowest bid he had to cut corners making the buildings unsafe which they soon discovered when someone drove a truck into the building with lots of explosives. The building wasn't destroyed but a lot of people lost their lives, so they had to make changes to the buildings. Even with all the new changes they were not ready for what was to come.

Here is something else I found strange. Each floor was made in an open concept. In other words they didn't want columns. In order to do this they had to make the outer walls stronger. Here's the strange part. Near the end of the documentary they said the columns got over heated from the flames and buckled inward. What columns? There were no columns.

When I was watching all this on TV, I got the impression that the planes hit the towers and within a few minutes the towers collapsed. Not so. What happened was that between the time the planes hit the building there were at least twelve hours, in which time all the people that were on the unaffected floors were able to escape.

Wouldn't it have been easier to make one building 50 stories high and wider and longer instead of two building 107 stories high? They would not have to compensate for the wind swaying the building or planes flying into it. Wider and shorter is better than narrow and tall. Like Spock would say, "That's just logical." I think all this was, was a bunch of men trying to compensate for small penises. That's what the other Spock would say or Freud.

— Emile (*not an architect*) Fougere

CHOSE WISELY, JEDI

Do you know how many forces there are in the universe? Neither do I but there are many. I never said I was a genius. Do you know which two are the most powerful? That much I do know. The two most powerful forces are...... wait for it. Positivity and negativity. They both have the power to change people and the world. Most people in general live their lives in a negative state (that's not a place but a state of mind). Can you pick which of these is positive and which is negative. A peace rally or an an-ti war rally. A pro-life rally or an anti-abortion rally. If you rally for pease you get pease, if you rally for anti-war you get more war, if you rally for life you get life, if you rally for an-ti abortion you get more abortions. Remember, two wrongs don't make a right and two negatives don't make a positive. Every time you think negative thoughts you draw more negativity to you. Every time you talk negative with someone you not only bring more negativity to yourself but you send it to others. Here's a thought, wouldn't two rights make a right and wouldn't two positives make a positive. Think about that, really think about it. You can't go wrong with that kind of logic. The more positive thoughts you have about your health the healthier you can become. The more positive thoughts you have about your financial situation the better that will get. This and many aspects of your life can change just by the way you think. So, stay positive.

— Emile (*may the force be with you*) Fougere

THINKING

Are you a thinker? You may not think you are but you are, we all are. It's like dreaming, you may not think you dream but you do. Some things you have to think about but some things you don't need too. Like breathing, chewing, hearing not the same as listening, seeing not the same as looking. When you eat you have to think about what you eat and how much you eat. It's the same thing when it comes to drinking but more so, especially when it comes to liquor. If you drink too much liquor thats when your brain shuts off and if it doesn't, later on you might wish it had.

I don't know about you but I do my best thinking when I first get up in the morning but if I'm not careful I can do my worst thinking without even realizing it, especially if I just had a bad dream or if I wake up in pain or if I'm sick. There are so many things that can come into play when it comes to your thinking. Right now I'm thinking (overtime), I have to if I want to write this article. Before I go to karaoke I have to think about what I'm going to sing. When I play my guitar I have to think about what I'm going to play and as I play I have to think about the chords I'm going to play. The tricky part, you have to think about both hands at once. If you think that might be hard try drumming. You have to think about what your left hand is going to do plus what your right hand is going to do. It doesn't stop there, you have to think about what both feet are going to do. Then you have think about which drum your going to hit and when and how often. I don't know if you were thinking about learning to play drums or guitar, don't worry your brain can handle it. As a matter of fact your brain can handle anything, well almost anything except a blow to the head or drugs. Just to be on the safe side, I think everyone should wear a helmet and stay away from drugs. Just say yes and no. If you are reading this you're probably thinking I should stop thinking before I hurt myself. My motto is, "If your going to think, at least be productive". I know what your thinking, "Is this guy ever going to shut up". "Noooooo!" If this thought got you thinking my job is done and so am I.

— Emile (*this is too much fun to stop*) Fougere

FALSE ADVERTISING

How do you feel about advertising? I know that I am getting more and more skeptical every day. It's one think to go looking for something on line but it's another thing when they come looking for you. Did you know that your computer is monitoring every thing you type on your computer especially if your looking for something specific. Try it. Type in guitar or wrinkle cream or constipation and you will start getting advertisements for all those things. There must be a lot of people who type the word diabetes because every second ad has to do with diabetes. They say that your computer has a video camera in it and it can see everything you do. They must be able to see the big S on my forehead. I don't even walk in front of my computer naked anymore. So don't even try to find me. If you know what I look like you're probably not looking anyway. Talk about false advertising.

Here's an advertisement I fell for hook line and sinker. Guess which one. I'll give you three guesses and the first two don't count and no it's not pills for penis growth or Viagra if those were you first two guesses. It was something to cure Diabetes, help with tremors, ED and a few other things related to Diabetes. When I got the pills this is what it said on the bottle, "These statements have not been evaluated by the food and drug administration.

This drug is not intended to diagnose, treat, cure or prevent any disease." That's why I bought it, Daaaaah. Then I looked at the ingredients, looks like the ingredients for jellybeans, orange jellybeans. I guess I'll be asking for my money back. I know, good luck with that.

— Emile (*I know, I know, big S*) Fougere

NOT WRITTEN IN STONE

Is your life written in stone? I don't think so. What happens in your life depends mostly on choice. What you are and who you are was your choice. As a matter of fact you can even change your mind anytime in your life and some have, even me. I've changed professions, I've changed lifestyles and I've even changed wives, (not necessarily my choice). Like I said not everything is written in stone. Not everything is hereditary, I'm not even sure if anything is . Well maybe your looks or your hair colour. I'm not too sure about male pattern baldness. If you make a choice that turns bad and you say it's hereditary, that's just a cop-out. If you chose to smoke and get cancer is it really hereditary? When I was younger I choose to smoke, did I smoke because my parents smoked? No. I smoked by choice. Twenty years later I choose to quit, (not written in stone). There are people in prisons who choose crime , they new the consequences but choose it anyway. Even this was not written in stone, typing was hard enough without chiselling it in stone. There are many examples of people who turned their lives around by choice. At any time in your life you have the choice to change anything in your life (even your hair color) even male pattern baldness (Rogaine)???

I believe this but, I can't prove it except by my life. Most people start developing Alzheimers early in their life but without too many symptoms. Even when the symptoms become more noticeable people find it hard to accept. "Pride goeth before a fall." I'm glad my pride wasn't written in stone. I believe I had developed Alzheimers and the changes I made helped to slow down and even reversed it. I can see and feel the changes every day. I'm not saying I'm cured but it sure feels like it. Knock on stone. Check back with me when I turn one hundred.

— Emile (*no, I'm not stoned*) Fougere

I SPY WITH MY LITTLE EYE

The eye is a pretty remarkable thing to say the least and even sometimes strange. There are people that are colour blind not to be confused with not seeing colours the way they actually are. I saw a video on You Tube about how it's possible for two or more people to look at, let's say, a dress with one or more colours in it, not everyone will agree on which color or colors they see. How it is possible? Well, the colors of that dress can change depending on a change of background. Talk about your eyes playing tricks on you. I'll give you another example of optical illusions. One day I was driving in a car, I wasn't the driver otherwise we probably would have gotten into an accident. Anyway, we were passing this transport truck and I was looking at his tires and it looked like the truck was about six inches of the ground. Weird right?Another time I was driving down the highway during a snow storm and I was staring ahead, and after a while it looked and felt like I was going backwards, I had to blink otherwise I think I would have gone into a hypnotic trance. Plus it felt like the snowflakes were getting bigger. Has that ever happened to you? If your reading this and your from Florida there's a good chance it hasn't. Here's another thing. Have you ever noticed when your watching TV and there are two people in the same frame but one person is closer to the camera than the other, one of those people is more out of focus than the other but when the camera tries to focus on the other person the other person goes out of focus. Well, our eyes do the same thing. Try this, look at an object in front of you and you'll notice that everything else in front of you will go out of focus. Better yet, you can't see things behind you, unless you have eyes in the back of your head. In order to see everything else in focus you have to switch your gaze to what you want to look at one at a time. For example if I look at the word time that I just typed, I see it but I can't make out anything else on the page, their a blur. It's the same thing when your driving down the road, it's important that you keep your eyes on the road. There are so many distractions everywhere which explains why there are so many accidents. If your a passenger it's not always a good idea to say, "Look at that." A recipe for disaster. As I look at my computer I can see it clearly but at the same time there's a clock two feet away from me to my left. I can see it but I can't see what time it is, unless I move my head or eyes slightly. It's not tunnel vision, tunnel vision is the ability to see everything that's right in front of you but, just what is in front of you. Even if you wear glasses it doesn't make any difference. Seeing is believing.

— Emile (*focus, focus, focus*) Fougere

DO YOU HEAR WHAT I HEAR?

Do you know the difference between deaf and hard of hearing? Do you know the difference between hearing and listening? If you're deaf you can't hear anything and if you're hard of hearing you have trouble hearing certain sounds or people. Sometimes it's not always deaf or hard of hearing, it's selective hearing. Yes dear. Sometimes you can hear what someone is saying your just not listening. Yes dear. Sometimes it's just a matter of not understanding. If someone has an accent or slurs his words it can happen. Not everyone has perfect diction like me. It takes a lifetime to master. In my case I'm hard of hearing. My girlfriend got tired of hearing me say "what" all the time. I got hearing aids now she's getting tired of me saying, "stop yelling." When we go out to play cards or karaoke I have to take off my hearing aids. Way too loud. Can't win. Now when someone says something I just nod my head and say yes. I just hope it's nothing important, or I'm not quizzed on it later. If I am quizzed on something I just say "I don't remember you telling me that." I have a bad memory to boot. How convenient. I use'd see TV shows in which someone who was hard of hearing would talk louder than usual, I don't do that, do I? The only time I do that is if the other person is deafer than me. When someone is talking to me it helps if I can see their lips. I can't read lips but it does help. I know for a fact because during Covid I had a harder time hearing people when they had masks on. You know what would be good. If people came with subtitles. Maybe I'll invent glasses that writes down everything people say on a small screen on your glasses. Don't steal my idea now.

— Emile (*WHAT*) Fougere

FEAR OF LIVING VS FEAR OF DYING

Are you the kind of person who has a fear of dying. The older you get the more you have that fear. It's only natural, it's called Thanatophobia. Did you know that? First I heard of it. Here's another new one, Koinophobia, the fear of living (an ordinary life). There are many reasons to have a fear of dying, if you drive in heavy traffic, if you live in a dangerous neighborhood, when you go off to war, when you swallow a chicken bone, when your constipated.Of course when your constipated you may not have a fear of death, you just wish you were dead. When I say a fear of living I don't mean (an ordinary life). What I mean is that there are so many things that we do that are now thought of as bad for you. Micro-wave ovens, the utensils we use for cooking, what we eat, where we eat, sleeping, computers, TV, cell phones, the water we drink, air conditioners the list goes on and on and on. The next thing you know, it will be dangerous to use the toilet and it probably is if you have a small butt. I once heard that sneezing was bad for women, it causes over enlarged breasts. Too bad that doesn't work for men, I don't mean breast wise. If you didn't get it I meant penis. Got it? I miss the good old days when we lived dangerously and we didn't care or worry about it. By the way worrying is bad for your health too.

— Emile (*live a little*) Fougere

STOOL

Here's a shitty subject. Why is it if I say fart people smile or laugh, but if you say shit people turn up their nose. Poop is not as bad but still not funny. Have you ever been given a prescription for some sickness you have and the paper that comes with it says "may cause diarrhea or constipation." How is that even possible? I know, I know they don't mean both at the same time. I knew of a man who could tell what was wrong with your car by looking at your tail pipe. Pretty cool right? Well, there are doctors that can tell whats wrong with you by looking at your poop. Not cool if your the doctor. Not a job I would relish. They would have to pay me a lot to take that job. Imagine your on a date and (he or she) asks you, "What do you do for a living?"

I also read that if your poop floats it means something, (I don't remember what), probably bullshit. If it sinks it means something else. What does it mean when half sinks and half floats? That would be a big dilemma, don't you think? Sink or swim. I also read that the perfect color for shit is brown like cardboard. Isn't that just peachy. I just thought of another word for poop, "crap." Everything you always wanted to know about poop but were afraid to ask. That's it for now I need to go for a crap. Don't wait for me.

— Emile (*sorry for dumping on you*) Fougere

SYMPTOMS

Hi, how are you? That's a good question that we hear a lot, the problem sometimes is, the answer. The answer usually is "fine." My favourite usually is, 110%. Where the problem lies is that sometimes if you are with that person long enough the conversation shifts to health problems. Do you know why? For lack of a better subject to talk about, because it's hard to come up with a better topic. Usually when we do come up with another topic, believe it or not the other topics are negative too. Unless you have some good news to share. That is something that is rare.

Back to the topic at hand, "Symptoms." When you go to the doctor, normally we go with a problem, right? And you also go for a solution, right? A simple solution, right? And usually you expect a prescription, right? But, what if the doctor says, "Exercise and eat better" what would you do then? You would probably be dumbfounded and shocked, right again, not a question. Well, you know my medical history, I know boring. Did you also know that when we go to the doctor it's not to fix the problem, per say, but to stop the symptoms. And it seems that the only way to stop the symptoms is with PILLS. Guess what, with each pill comes more symptoms (side effects). Isn't that fun? From what I've seen and heard plus my experience, that's the way it is and it's not going to change any time soon. To get rid of most problems, sorry to say, it's exercise and proper eating habits. Not all problems can be fixed these ways. I have found other ways that can help with problems, if exercise and proper eating don't work. I, personally have tried these and I guarantee they worked for me. Do you wan't to know? Vitamins directed to each problem, acupressure, massage therapy and acupuncture. There is an acupressure point for just about anything that ails you. Acupuncture works but it can be expensive. I know, I tried it. The best part is there are no side effects. If you have any, and mean any health problems you can find one of these solutions on You Tube.

— Dr. Emile (*just kidding*) Fougere

DO, DO, DO, DO. DO, DO, DO, DO.

What's in this book may be very revealing to you or it may be very related to you, as one person put it or it may be just some thing very amusing. I've been told by some who I have given a sneak preview to, that it's philosophical and humorous. It didn't start that way. It started as just my thoughts on what was happening in the world concerning Corona Virus and the vaccine. Once that got boring, and I was enjoying what I was doing, then I couldn't stop even though it wasn't easy. I don't know who or what was pushing me but the thoughts kept coming and I couldn't stop them. Thoughts for my next book have already started. I don't know how long it will take but the thoughts seem to be coming faster and faster. Considering how fast the world is changing my next book may be more serious and less (as my girlfriend puts "comical.") I'm not sure at this point. You'll have to wait and see. I'll have to wait and see. Don't you just love a good mystery? I might even have a spot or two in it from other people, if I can get his or her or their approval.

I also have another book in the works (not THOUGHTS) that you may or may not like depending on your likes. A subject that you might even like to participate in. I'll give you a clue, it's mentioned in this book. There have been many people who have written books on the subject who will want to comment on (negative or positive) which will probable spark another book on the subject. You'll just have to wait and see. Hell, I'll even have to wait and see. I know, I can't wait either.

— Emile (*do, do, do, do*) Fougere

WHO'S REALLY IN CHARGE?

Have you ever wondered about that question? In charge of what, you may ask? Who's in charge when it comes to you? Who's in charge when it comes to this world? I'm not even going to try to answer those questions. I'm just trying to make you think about these questions. When you go to work, who's in charge? Your boss? If it's your business is it you or is it your customers? At home is it you or your spouse or your children? Every home is different. When it comes to your town or city or country, who's really in charge? Is it president, a prime minister, a king, a queen? Or, are they just puppets of some organization? I heard it said that the whole world is controlled by the Pope. Imagine that. I know that the Pope is in charge of the Catholic church, but the world? I also heard that all governments are controlled by a group of the wealthiest people in the world. That I **might** believe, but it's just speculation or rumors, not on my part. Imagine imperfect humans in charge of an imperfect world. What could possibly go wrong. I don't have the answer and I'm not sure if I want to know the answer. It scares me just thinking about it. A meteor wiped out the dinosaurs, but it looks like we might wipe ourselves out long before the next meteor hits.

A lot of these so called leaders may have had good intentions when they started *maybe* but if they are not really in charge, or if power really does corrupt then all the good intentions in the world goes out the window.

Millions of people through out time have given their time and even their resources to bring freedom and justice to this world but yet here we are. I ask the question again, "Who **is** in charge?"

— Emile (*good thing I'm not in charge*) Fougere

EMOTIONS

Emotions are all part of everyones life, good or bad. It starts the minute we are born. The first thing we do is cry, then we move on from there. Next we laugh or smile when something makes us happy. We get mad when someone does something we don't like. We get jealous when someone has something we don't, especially money. The reason I bring up the topic of emotions is to help you to learn how we can control them. I've mentioned before the importance of changing your negative thoughts into positive thoughts, well the same can be done with emotions, for the most part, unless you stub your toe or bump your head. That's when the four letter words come out. The same is true when someone you love dies, then the tears start to flow. Nothing wrong with that. The problem lies when we take it too far to the point of obsession. Emotions can be trained the same as thoughts. It's not always easy but with persistence anything is possible. If not, then you maybe, just maybe it could affect your health, even to the point of death. Hate is another emotion that can be bad for you. Believe it or not hate is more harmful to yourself than to the person you are hating. As a matter of fact the person you hate may not know or care that you hate them. Talk about a waste of hate. Then you end up hating yourself for being so stupid for wasting all that time hating them.

What a pity, another emotion that may be a waste of time especially if you pity yourself. Pitying someone else not so bad. The most useless and most harmful emotion is anger, unless you want a heart attack or ulcers.

Here is an emotion that is worth pursuing, LOVE. Better than any drug known to man. Talk about a high, especially your first love. There is nothing like it, not even the love of money. Protect it at all cost.

The best way to fight negative emotions is with positive thoughts, positive affirmations and even meditation. What do you have to lose. Nothing ventured, nothing gained.

— Emile (*go for it*) Fougere

BS

There's an expression: "Bullshit makes the grass grow greener." Actually, that's all bullshit is good for. It has no medicinal purpose, it won't help you lose weight, it won't help clear your complexion and it doesn't go good on your salad I don't care what anyone tells me. Not even a priest or minister. You can't believe what everyone tells you. Check it out for your self, do research. I heard a comedian jokingly say, "If you heard it three times, it must be true." I get bombarded with BS everyday, no BS. Why is it wrong to say bullshit but it's alright to say BS? We all know what BS means. I think I know why. That's what parents started doing when they didn't want their children to know what they were saying , in this case (BS) they were to lazy to spell the whole word.

Speaking of lazy, a lot of the ADS on TV (now you got me doing it) are directed at lazy people. "Take this pill and you'll lose weight in no time." If you want to lose weight stop eating so much and stop eating junk food. "If you want to look like a body builder take *this* pill." If you want to look like Arnold go to the GYM. I knew this young man years ago, he was tall and skinny, then all of a sudden he was buff. Turns out he started taking steroids. It did the trick but at what cost. Nothing in life is that easy, easy usually comes at a cost. Unless your the bullshitter, better known as conmen. Don't get me wrong, I have fallen victim a few times, OK many times. I've learned my lesson, the delete button is there for a reason and now I'm getting pretty good at using it. The word delete is worn out on my keyboard. If you believe that I have some land in Florida I'd like to sell you. Where did I put my hip waders? Just kidding, or am I ????

At what point in history did doctors become pill pushers? I guess helping people wasn't enough or didn't pay enough, Getting paid in eggs and chickens didn't cut it. You can only eat so many eggs. By the way eggs are good for you, better than pills. If you go on u-tube and ask, "What are the side affects of eggs?" There is no long list. Zilch, nota. Now medications, that's another story, no BS. Would I try to con you? Wink, wink.

— Emile (*the cat is out of the bag*) Fougere

WHO'S HEALTH IS IT ANYWAY?

Should you leave your health totally in someone else's hands? When it comes to our health we have so many choices. Medication, vitamins, herbs, meditation, yoga, tai chi, the list goes on and on, (this is my way of saying I don't know them all). Do your own research. You're allowed to. There's no law against that (yet). Some people (doctors) may say there should be a law or at least a rule. What is or should be the most important thing in your life? Health or a bigger TV. Health or a bigger house? Health or... you know what I'm getting at? Only you can make that choice; choose wisely.

— Emile (*Just say no*) Fougere

COMMUNICATION

Communication is a very complex and complicated thing.

It seems that everyone has their own way of communicating, especially when it comes to writing books. Why do more educated people write books that only more educated people can read? Don't they think that I would like to know what they are talking about? It is possible to convey what they are trying to say without using big fancy words. If you can translate english into , let's say French, then is it not possible to translate English into English? Reading is how we become more educated. It's been said that after finishing school many people stop reading all together, pity. They don't know what they're missing. I may not ever be able to read every book ever written but at least I'm making an effort. To do that I would have to live a long time. Since there are books still being written it would take forever unless you can speed read. I don't speed read, I turtle read.

Surveys: I was reading a book on surveys written by a University professors, not an easy read on my best day. Words I have never even heard before. Who are they trying to impress? Thank goodness for Seri, easier than a dictionary. Best invention ever. I don't swear and I don't do genius. Don't be so surprised. Here's an idea, make reading easy for the average person. Simplify, simplify, simplify. For some people you may as well be speaking a different language. Survey that! I know medical and scientific jargon is not always easy but I'm sure it can be. Unless, unless maybe they don't want you to understand. Simplicity is the answer. If you can't understand my book, I've failed. If you think this book is hard, don't get me started on instruction manuals. Now, there's a can of beans you don't want to open.

— Emile (*I love to read*) Fougere

DIABETES

Before I go into any detail I must tell you I'm not a doctor. Nor do I claim to know more than doctors. A lot of what I do know I've gleamed from books on medicine. What I am saying is I am diabetic and being diabetic I have learned a lot about diabetes that I think has helped me to control it, so far, to some degree. I don't think I'm ready to give up my Free Style Libre just yet, but maybe some day or maybe not at all. Actually it's always nice to know where I am with my diabetes and it keeps me in check, so to speak. Better to be safe than sorry. I still trust and need the medical profession to some degree. Like I've mentioned before, I'm not a big believer in medication and if you knew me you'd know why. I still take my insulin mainly because it has no side effects so far. I do believe dieting has benefits, not only what you eat but mostly how much you eat. I know there are people out there that can eat what they want and as much as they want. I'm happy for you, the thing is I was one of you at one time. I was not always diabetic but I was probably predisposed to it. Not probably, I was. Diabetes is like Russian roulette, it's not something anyone should play with. Lesson learned, too little but not too late. I am writing this to help you avoid some of the pitfalls that are out there. There are a lot of charlatans out there who will do and say anything to convince you they have a cure, and I've heard them all (not just on the subject of diabetes). Here's one I heard just yesterday, that Alzheimers is caused by the way you sleep. I'm gullible, but not that gullible. I guess you could say I've done the research for you. Your welcome. I guess you could also say "I've been a fool for you." Literally. Hey, that should be my theme song.

I cannot stress this enough, moderation is one of the keys to prevention and or cure. If you put this into practice you are well on your way to a happier life. Do not just believe me, prove it to yourself. It's your life. Hopefully a longer life.

— Emile (hope springs eternal) Fougere

LOVE & MARRIAGE + KIDS

Why do people get married and have kids? When you look at all the divorces in the world and all the troubled kids it's not hard to see why. You've heard of love at first sight. That's a load of crock, it's more like lust at first sight. You can't learn much about someone in a bar, and if you did because of the booze you probable forgot everything. All you know at this point is that you both like to party and drink and probably have sex. I knew a lady who had a daughter who liked to party every week-end. She started dating this guy and they soon got married. Two months later they were divorced. The problem started when he wanted to settle down and stop partying. She loved the parties and the drinking. She left. Good thing there were no kids involved. Moral of the story is you can't learn about someone in a bar. Reminds me of the story of the woman who was married to an alcoholic. She didn't know he was an alcoholic until he came home sober one day.

If you are versed in what you do weather it's your job, marriage or raising kids you may not succeed. Affection is crucial in a marriage and for raising kids. Attention is important too. Affection & Attention. If you are not willing to give these two things don't get married. It's a full time job. Just saying.

When it comes to marriage and having kids things have to change or nothing will change. People need to know about certain things (before) embarking on a journey like this. Marriage and rearing kids should be something that should be taught in school or at church or by successful parents. If you don't know anything about the person you are dating, that's a recipe for disaster. To get a marriage licence you should have to pass a test like when you get a drivers licence. In this case you can't get a beginners license. Like a drivers license there should be a questionnaire and a test. If you come from a dysfunctional family, that's what you will bring into your new family. When I was going out with my first wife we went to see a priest and he asked us if there was anything we didn't like about the other. Without thinking my fiance said, "He snores." At this point the priest said, "How do you know?" Then I said, "She could hear me from the other room when I visited her at her parent's home." That was a close call. When answering the questionnaire it's important that you be honest.

Once you get all the questions answered and you've learned everything you (need) to know about each other and their family, then you have a foundation to work from. And if one or both of you want to move forward and one or both of you have issues to work on then it's important to go for counseling. Next, once you have worked out all your issues then you can start building on (that) foundation. All this advice can also be applied to people wanting to live together. Don't worry be happy, that's an order.

— Emile (*lived and learned the hard way, twice*) Fougere

LEAVE ME ALONE!!!!!

There's something I hear my girlfriend say a lot (not to me and especially not in bed) and the word *garbage*. When something is not working to her satisfaction (again not me) she says garbage. In other words this is going in the garbage. My point, when it comes to some of the massages I get on e-mail or facebook (leave me alone) the most used key on my computer is delete. You would not believe how many e-mails and posts I get about diabetes. Everybody and his brother has a cure for diabetes. Don't get me started on erectile disfunction. Now that's a hard subject. I know some men don't like that subject. Don't go soft on me now. Another crapy subject, diarrhea don't run away. Just today I received an e-mail on constipation. How did they know I was constipated? Shit happens and so does constipation. By the way did you hear the one about the constipated mathematician? He worked it out with a pencil. Now a days they use calculators, I wonder how that would work? Let's get off this shitty subject, please, delete.

It seems everyone wants to be my friend on facebook. Why? They don't even know me and what's worse, even the ones that are already my facebook friends are asking me to be friends and they tell me how I can get $250,000 for free from the American gov ernment.Leave me alone!!!!!! SCAM? You bet. There are doctors out there that keep telling me all the foods that are bad for you. It looks like the only food that's good for you is broccoli. Bon appetite. Did you hear, that if you sleep the wrong way you can develop Alzheimer's? Bonsoir.

— Emile (*FO to the scammers & bullshitters*) Fougere

TOTALLY CONFUSED

Yes, I'm confused. We have gone through many changes since time began. We have gone through the stone age, the bronze age etc... I can't think of all of them but it'll come to me. Right now I think we are living in the age of confusion. The biggest, I believe is religious. I checked with Siri and she told me that their are more than 10,000. WOW!!! No wonder people are confused including me. I was born Catholic then I switched to another. After all that is said and done I ended up with more questions than answers. There are five types of people in the world, people who believe in God, Atheists, the undecided, people who don't care one way or the other and Agnostics. If I left anyone out I'm sorry. Let me be more specific about my confusion concerning religion. I'm not saying I'm right I'm just saying I'm confused. So please don't get me wrong.

1. When Cain killed Able and was banished from where he was living for killing his brother eventually he got married and had kids. I know Adam & Eve probably had more children that eventually ended up moving to where Cain was but the Bible doesn't say that. I suppose the Bible is thick enough without adding too much detail but it might have answered a few questions.

2. When the Tower of Babel fell the Bible says that the peoples languages were confused and they could not understand each other. It seems to me it wasn't just their languages that were confused. Because now we not only have over 10,000 religions but we also have over 7,000 languages. Plus (as if things weren't confusing enough) we have different colors. Did you know that at one time black people were the dominant species? It's even been said that Adam and Eve were black. Sorry white supremacists , not my words. Revolution can sure turn things upside down. I hope we are not on the verge of a new revolution and if we are I hope it's a revolution towards equality. Of course, there are more orientals in the world now than any other race, so watch out world. And they know marshal arts. Just saying. Hayaa.

3. In the Bible it says that some people lived to be almost 1000 years old just before the great flood, but now we only live on average (well not quite average) of no more than 100 years. Some scholars say that they counted time differently back then. According to them that would mean that either the days were a LOT longer and the earth was spinning slower or people were having children when they were only 5 years old. Talk about robbing the cradle. Do any of these scenarios make sense to you? Me neither. I'm not a scholar, but I'm no fool. After reading my other thoughts you might think, "that's debatable". Just don't say it, I have feelings too.

— Emile (*Count your blessings*) Fougere

THE PROS, NO, CONS OF READING, EXERCISE AND MEDITATION

I've been reading for quit a few years and there's a lot to be said for reading. It expands your horizons, it helps you learn may things like, how to survive, (which may be important soon), you can learn a lot about health and wellness. Plus it helps to replenish the neurons in your brain. If your car broke down on the highway would you just call an Uber and just leave it there on the side of the road? If you were rich, you might. I'm talking about the average person. NO! You would probable call a tow truck to give you a boost or bring it to the nearest garage to get it fixed. So, what do you do if someone you love has Alzheimers? Do you abandon them on the side of the road, so to speak? I did, and only because they were too far gone AND I DIDN'T KNOW THEN WHAT I KNOW NOW. When it comes to people that is not always the case, in some cases in the beginning there are steps that can be taken to help or even reverse Alzheimer's to some degree.

I would venture to guess that mental and brain problems (which is basically the same thing) started around the time the television was invented. When it comes to your brain, one thing is important when it comes to brain health is your ability to imagine. When it comes to watching TV no brain power or imagination is required. Nothing is left to the imagination. You become a zombie during that time. Don't get me wrong, I watch TV, as a matter of fact, when I was young I was addicted to TV and we only had two stations, YES TWO. But, one of the things that is most beneficial to brain health is reading. I did not know this before, and I believe it now.Exercise is number two on that list and there's more. All this has been proven with rats and monkeys, which I do not approve of. It's petty hard to get a monkey to read a book, anyway. And if you can, can you get them to read my book? Just a thought. And one more thing Meditation. If you start all three of these things by at least 65 years of age or earlier I guarantee you will feel and be better.

Reading: 1hr/ day.

Exercise: 1hr/day, ask Arnold.

Meditation: 1/2hr / day. Tibetan Monks don't get Alzheimer's

Stay away from medications.

Don't waste time or time will waste you, guaranteed. What do you have to lose? Hell, what do you have to gain? I'll tell you, a longer life, better quality of life and you might even remember your life or whats left of it.

If you suspect you or someone you love has Dementia or Alzheimers, get with the program. If you do try it and you find it works spread the word. A few hours of prevention is worth a lifetime of cure. I know, believe me I know.

— Emile (*patient #1*) Fougere

UNITED WE STAND

I'm sure most people know how the rest of that quote goes. That's a high ideal. We are living in a world where unity looks impossible and if you think that way you are probably right. There's another saying, "Nothing is impossible." I'd like to believe that as much as the next guy. Someone once asked the question, "What would you do if you had a billion dollars," I said I would help the homeless, the poor, the hungry and people with Alzheimer's. And I would, but it still would not unite us and it would still not solve all problems. Even if I had 10 billion dollars, do you know what would happen? Someone with 20 billion dollars would kill me and take the money. Because rich people are never satisfied. Since I don't, I feel pretty safe. With that kind of money you could make a lot of worthwhile changes, but we are still stuck with disunity. So what prevents us (the world) from having unity? Good question.

I saw a movie years ago called "Dave." It's story about a school teacher who looked like the president of the United States. The president was too sick to perform his duties and his board of directors thought the country would go to pot (not literally), so they brought Dave to the white house to take his place until the president was better. As the president he started implementing changes. The board was not happy and he soon found out who was really in charge. I don't know how true this is but there are small minorities of billionaires who run and own everything. Banks, industries, governments you name it they own it. Did you know that the house you own is not really yours? If the government wanted to take your house tomorrow they could and theres nothing you could do about it, ask Jackie Vautour and many others. Sure they will try to buy you out, but if you don't accept they'll just take it anyway.

We've had wars, we've had revolutions, we've had protests and still no unity. The billionaires are not the world, the people are and that's where the power lies that's where the unity can be. The world now has the ability to unite more than ever because we are more connected now than any other time in history. I'm not saying revolt, I'm saying unite and take a stand for peace and unity. Then we can have the kind of world that benefits everyone.

Like I said at the beginning, "Nothing is impossible."

— Emile (*Nothing*) Fougere

TEXTING

Have you ever tried texting someone? If you have you may have run into this. The phone gives you an option of what your next word should be and more often than not it is right. But sometimes it can be quite funny. Here are a few examples of what I mean:

I was typing this, 'The only way I would read a children's book is if I was reading to a, The phone gave me this option, not "child" but "chicken." If I was reading to a chicken. The word child was not even on the list of options.

— Emile (*Oh my dog*) Fougere

THE ENGLISH LANGUAGE

The english language is pretty complex when you think about it. The funniest part that I mean is certain words are spelt the same but mean different things and the only way you know which thing is being referred too is by the context. Here are a lot of examples:

Tape: Electrical tape, tape recorder, scotch tape, measuring tape, the verb tape and even then you have to be specific. You can't just say "hand me the tape."

String: Guitar string, string quartet, string graph, string theory, string me a tale. Take out your dictionary and look through it and I bet you will find literally thousands of words that have more than one meaning. Couldn't they have come up with a different word?

Ring: Wedding ring, engagement ring, ring of truth, ring a bell, ring tone.

Stool: Shit, poop, dump, number two, more than a fart, do do, crap.

Crap: A crap table, is that something you shit on?

Climax: That word has more than one meaning if you know what I mean. You know. Yes, I'm talking about a climax in a book. What were you thinking? Get your mind out of the gutter. While you there get mine out too.

Dogs: Canine, mutt, man's best friend and that's not counting the different kinds of dogs.

House: home, dwelling, building, shelter, shack.

Here's a new twist, same word different language.

Fuck: In french, fuck is a seal, don't get the two mixed up, like a fuck of approval or fucked with a kiss and never f##k a seal. I'm not swearing, I'm talking about seals

Did you know that the word fuck is an acronym for Fornication Under Consent of the King: In medieval England a person was not allowed to have sex unless he had the consent of the king. If it was by the consent of the pope then it would be FUCP.

Here's another one: **Swear**, I swear I was talking about seals. I would swear on a stack of Bibles. Another one: **Stack:** She's stacked, stack of pancakes, stack those boxes

Breasts: Boobs: tits, hooters, knockers.

Foul: Chicken, foul ball, foul- to make a mistake, foul mouth.

Here's a good one. I saw this cartoon in a paper a long time ago. Picture this: An Italian soldier is laying on the ground all bloodied and cut up and there's an American soldier standing over him and he says, "When you said it's a mine, I thought you meant it's a yours." Two words spelt the same but two different meanings. Talk about consequences.

Something else they do to the english language. They shorten the words or turn them into anagrams. Do u no what I mean. United states is now U.S.. Here's my not so favorite: Emojis, a whole new language.

— Emile (*What the F**k*) Fougere

DEPRESSION

There is nothing funny about depression, as a matter of fact the opposite is true. I'm not a doctor or any kind of health professional. I've done a lot of research on the subject and all I can do is give my five cents on the subject. Five cents is not much but it's something. I'll tell you right now that medication is not the answer and many doctors would probably agree with me. But many doctors believe in the pharmaceutical god, or Big Pharma. The brain is a very fragile thing and pumping it with any kind of drugs is not the answer. When it comes to depression, drugs may have been a contributing factor. Let's face it when we have problems, weather is was self inflicted or inflicted by someone else, a lot of people turn to drugs or if their problems cause psychological problems then they are sent to a doctor, who prescribe medications, after that it's all downhill from there. Just saying. Do I have the answer? I don't know. What I say can't be any worse. Opinions are like noses, everyone has one. If you are depressed, it's probably started with your own negative thinking. That's how it always starts. Been there done that. Probably not to the extent that you may be, but I was on that road. The thing is, before I got too far along on that road I decided to get off and you can too. The first thing you need to do is to decide to get off that road. The next thing you need to do is to start thinking positive things about yourself. They're there, you just need to look for them, instead of all the negative things you've been telling yourself. They're all lies and you know it. If you can't think of anything nice to say about yourself, don't say anything at all. If you find that hard, do what I did and believe me it works. Positive meditation videos, believe me there are hundreds of them on you tube. If that doesn't block the negative nothing will and they're free. Say no to drugs and medication, as if there's a difference. Thinking something does not make it true, and if it is true, nobody is perfect. When you do meditate, do deep breathing exercises with it. Everything helps. The problem is the brain, so do the things that help the brain. Did you know that physical exercise is good for the brain? If you are not able to exercise physically, exercise mentally as if your were exercising physically. It takes a lot of practice with the same results without sweating. Here is what you do, sit in your favorite chair for as much time as it would normally take you to do exercises and imagine doing each exercise. The brain doesn't know the difference. Well it does and it doesn't if you know what I mean. It's the same thing when it comes to positive thinking. If you tell yourself your smart or happy, you're brain doesn't know the difference, it reflects on what your telling it. To summarize: Exercise is good for you, positive thoughts are good for you, meditation is good for you and medication and drugs is bad for you. Just my opinion. Take it or leave it. I'm just being honest.

— Emile (*Get with the program*) Fougere

THEORY

Definition: A supposition or a system of ideas intended to explain something; especially one based on general principles independent of the thing to be explained. Like, "Darwins theory of evolution."

Now the key word here is "supposition."

Definition of supposition: An uncertain belief.

Now the key word here is "uncertain."

Definition of uncertain: Not able to be relied on; not known or definite.

Can you see what I'm getting at? They don't know for sure, and as long as they are not sure it remains a THEORY. This word is used a lot in science, in medicine and in many things. The written word is not always truth but many people put their reputations on the line just for the sake of selling books and the almighty dollar. Some have been discredited by someone else's opposing theory. Now the original guy with his original theory has gotten rich and now it's someone else's turn to get rich on the same idea until someone else debunks his idea. And the list goes on and on until maybe and I mean maybe somebody can prove this theory.

Don't hold your breath. Remember, "uncertain," not to be relied on.

I've noticed a few times, when I'm reading a book about something (medical or scientific) that sounds important, that sometimes they sneak in the words "hasn't been proven." Or words to that effect. That's just to cover their assess "just in case." I believe if someone has a "theory" and he or she is "uncertain," I think they should keep it to themselves until they **are** certain. Just my opinion, not a theory.

— Emile (*food for thought*) Fougere

MINI-THOUGHTS

FOR PEOPLE WHO HATE TO READ

I know who you are. You can't hide from me. Well I guess you can. I better keep this short

BULLSHIT

They say bullshit makes the grass grow greener but I don't think it does the same for the brain. For the last two years I have been keeping tabs on the covid statistics and up until yesterday they have been pretty good

WHO CAN YOU TRUST?

In the world we live in today

— Emile (*I'm drawing a blank*) Fougere

GUITARS

I am still puzzled with the seven stringed guitars that they keep showing on Facebook. Are they even seven stringed bass guitars or seven stringed rhythm guitars? And can you buy music lesson books to go with them? Do chords come with them?

By the way, do you know where I can buy a seven string guitar for my friend who has six fingers? Archie Bunkers wife bought Archie a guitar and he said I can't play that, it has six strings and I only have five fingers.

— Emile (*Clueless in Shediac*) Fougere

REHASHING

I'm going to be sending out some or all of my old thoughts again for those of you who might have missed them and I might be changing or adding a few points to them also.

— Emile (*Doo doo doo doo*) Fougere

CORONA VIRUS

I've been told for the third time that everyone will end up getting the corona virus when everything is said and done. It's been said that if you hear something three times it must be true. Even Dr. Fauci said it. If he said it...

— Emile (*I don't know*) Fougere

THE SOUNDS WE MAKE!!!!

Burp – sneeze – fart – cough. Who came up with these names anyway. I can see how they came up with the names burp and cough because they sound like their spelt. The word sneeze is spelt nothing like it sounds, it sounds more like achoo. Wow, I spelt it right, word check didn't correct me. Now fart is a different story, I tried to spell it and the best I could come up with is phhhhhhh You can't spell it but you can smell it. By the way spell check came up with this but they didn't come up with an alternative spelling either.

I have a question. Why do people excuse themselves when they burp, sneeze or cough but nobody excuses themselves when they fart. They just smile. That's the nature of the beast I guess.

— Emile (*phhhhhhhh*) Fougere

Did you just smile?

SHAKING ALL OVER

Hi everybody. I have a funny story I must share. It's no secret that I live with tremors. It's not the first time I've mentioned it. You might even be tired of hearing it but here's my story. When it comes to typing and texting it can be quite challenging, miss a letter here and miss a letter there or hit a letter more often than planed. Anyway yesterday we were on a bus tour and as you might imagine the roads were pretty bumpy to say the least. Noella was trying to compose a text and she turned to me and said, "It's pretty hard to write my text with all these pumps in the road." At which point I said, "Welcome to my world."

— Emile (*Come on that was funny*) Fougere

SPERL CHEQUE

Ive sed this many time that I have tremmers and Im knot godd at speilling , thas why I haave spel checkk. I misssa letars and I hittt too manie lettars. I twitc h an hit das rong latter an Im nott tooo goood at punktuation ether. The ting is even iff i didnt use spelll cheque u coud stl reed this. Rite? Dis is me siging offf.

— Emiliee (*did I got any ting write?*) Flougear

PAIN IS RELATIVE

I know I talk a lot about my health and I usually try to put a humorous spin on it, if you can't laugh at yourself who can you laugh at. Not that I would laugh at any of you. Remember, laughter is the best medicine. Here's the latest, I have sciatic nerve problems in my left leg. By itself it's not bad, it's the things I do that cause the pain. It hurts when I try to get up or sit down, when I cough, when I sneeze, when I fart and when I crap. I'd hate to think how bad it would be if I was constipated. If I have diarrhea, not a problem, no effort required.

— Emile (*ouch*) Fougere

TONE - DEAF

About 25 years ago I was driving my car and listening to the radio. I don't know if what the announcer was joking or not but he said that there was a band that was playing off key music that catered to tone deaf people. I thought what a novel idea. Not really. I know there are people who can't sing because they are tone deaf, but tone deaf listeners? I don't think so. Twenty-five years later and we have all kinds of tone-deaf singers, it's called KARAOKE. Not to say that all karaoke singers are bad or tone-deaf. You be the judge. Just saying.

— Emile (*one of the good ones*) Fougere

That's what I've been told. What do they know they're tone-deaf. The rest just wish they were deaf.

WHY? WHY? WHY?

I know the answer, I just said that for emphasis. Have you ever bought a cell phone? That was a stupid question, of course you have, everybody has. I would say even my grandfather has, but I AM the grandfather. In my long life (since cell phones have been invented) I would say I have had at least 5 cell phones, flip phones included. Each time I bought one the phone was a little bit bigger or smaller than my last one. So, because of that I had to also buy a new protective cover for it. To protect it for when you run over it with your jeep like someone I know (no name included). WHY? WHY? WHY?

Another thing, why is it every time you get a new phone the charging cord is different than the last five phones I had? WHY? WHY? WHY? The answer, MONEY. MONEY. MONEY. Plain and simple. Maybe not simple but plain.

— Emile (*give me a break*) Fougere

JOKES & FUNNY ANECDOTES

PROPER ETIQUETTE

What's the proper etiquette at a Thanksgiving dinner; who get the drumstick? Now at Thanksgiving dinner for cannibals; who gets the penis?

OH, CRAP!

Quark from Deep Space Nine was in the Hollow Deck cleaning the floor and he said: "Those stupid humans, I have to keep telling them, the toilets are not real."

STAR TREK

Captain Picard and Lieutenant Data were standing in the shuttle bay and there was a small borg craft there with the words carpet cleaners on the side.

Captain Picard said: "Data. Why did you hire them to clean our carpets". Data responded: "The ad in the paper said, "Resistance was futile.""

THE VOICE

Let me set the stage for this story (literally). Time: September 16/06/BC (Before Corona). I was at a bar, on stage singing karaoke. You know some times there's a break in the song. Well at this particular time, there was, and so I put the mic behind me and by accident I farted, rather loudly, into the mic. It just so happened that three people at the bar turned around and for a moment I thought I was on "The Voice."

SCAMMED AGAIN

I just bought this collection of the top 100 of Acapella Karaoke music. The only problem it's hard to know where one song starts and the next one begins. The good thing is I can turn it up as loud as I want and the neighbours don't complain. The only thing is, I can't help but think I might have been scammed.

MARK TWAIN

The famous writer Mark Twain, not related to Shenia Twain had been invited to this fancy ball, now he was known for being a bit of a heavy drinker so on this particular evening he was a bit tipsy. And this lady came up to him and said to him, "*Siiiir,* you are drunk," to which Mark said " Madam, you are Ugly, and tomorrow I shall be sober, but tomorrow you shall be still ugly."

MUZZY

I went to Karaoke one night with my son at the Salty Sea dog. The hosts name was Muzzy. I had sung a few songs during the night and after my last song I said to him. "There a lot of good singers here, do you ever get any bad ones." He said, "No, you're the first."

THIRD! REALLY?

I was in a karaoke contest one time, when I first started doing karaoke. I came in third and my son came in second and this young lady who could not even carry a tune came in first. Come to find out she was host's girlfriend. He did't last long as a host there for too much longer. The fact that the place burned down didn't help either. I said I came in third but I failed to mention that there were only three people in the contest.

KARAOKE

I was in this Legion a while back, it was karaoke night and there was this young man sitting there front and centre. Now that's what you call an Oxymoron (young man- Legion). Get it? Anyway, I tried.

I talked to him and asked if he sang and he told me he sang heavy metal and that's probably why he didn't put his name up.

A week later I went to another bar, can you guess why? Karaoke. Anywho, there were a lot of young people there so when I got up to sing I said, "Sorry, I don't do heavy metal." And there was this older couple there all dressed up and I looked at them and I said, "I don't do opera either." Do you know another thing that is an oxymoron? Karaoke and singing. Did you also know that karaoke is Japanese for tone deaf. That's ironic. Do I have to explain all these jokes?

BEAUTY IS IN THE EYE OF THE BEHOLDER

I just thought up of a new kind of art. First, what you do is eat two cans of beans unless you prefer cabbage rolls, then you get naked. Oh, don't forget the canvas. Then what you do is take out your paint (preferably tubes) either one colour at a time or mix 4 or 5 different colours in one tube. Here's the exciting part. You squirt the paint up your ass hole, then bend over the canvas. The rest is self explanatory. No video available. I'm calling it, you guessed it. FART ART. I'm joking, a dirty joke but none the less a joke.

LOL

One evening Noella and I went out to Barachois to a club, no not karaoke. They had a comedy show Noella wanted to see. It was in french, keep in mind my french is not so good. If you've read any of my posts neither is my english. Sorry, I'm rambling again. Anyway, back to my story. Noella is very vocal when it comes to laughing, no exaggeration. I'm not sure if it was the jokes or Noella laughing but people were laughing so much they had tears in their eyes. Even I was laughing hard and I didn't understand the jokes. Best night of my life. After the show the host of the show gave us free tickets to their next few shows. That was nice. I'm not sure but I think he had an ulterior motive. That last part is not true. It could happen.

BLOW HARD

I know someone, actually a few someones who have this problem. I won't mention any names. Here it is, when they blow their noses it can be quite intense. One afternoon I was in my kitchen talking with my insurance company and this person who shell remain nameless blew her nose. That should narrow it down. The insurance agent said, "You must live close to the highway." I asked "Why do you say that?" He said, "I just heard a transport." I don't kiss and tell so I just smiled and said, "Ah ha."

TWINS - Keep that in mind while you read this story

I know this guy who shall remain nameless (CC) who is a TWIN and someone asked him if it was hard for people to tell them apart. He said only when we go to a nude beach. I have a penis and my TWIN has a vagina. One day we were over at his place and his TWIN sister was there and the topic of age came up and he asked his TWIN sister how old she was. TWIN SISTER. **Dah.**

IT'S NOT A RECORD

I made a call today and was put on hold for two and one half hours. I thought it might be a Guinness book of world records but I was wrong. The record is held by a man from England who was put on hold by his wife in Australia. 15hrs, 40minutes and 1 second. I bet he was mad. She probably thought he was paying. Surprise, surprise. He reversed the charges. I didn't have to. It was a 1-800 #.

OUCH!!

I met a friend one day and he said, "I heard you were suffering with a pinch nerve in your leg, how are you now?" I said, "I'm alright now but it still hurts when I fart." Someone told me once that a pinched nerve in your leg can be caused by carrying your wallet in your back pocket. Made sense to me so I stopped carrying my wallet in my back pocket. And voila, no more pain. On the same note, I new a man who kept his wallet in his back pocket but he didn't have nerve pain problems. He took out his wallet one day and I noticed his wallet full of business cards that looked like he had been collecting since he was twelve years old. If he was suffering from anything it would be nose bleeds.

OLD PEOPLE HUMOR

I met this young man in the mall one day and we got to talking and the subject turned to sex. He asked me how old I was and I told him I was 74. He asked me, "At 74 how is the sex"? I asked him if he knew what metamorphosis was. He said, "Isn't that like when a caterpillar turns into a butterfly?" I told him, "Yes." He said, "What does that have to do with sex?"

I said, "When your young sex is fun, but when you get older it turns into work." "Another thing about sex when your older it takes longer to recover for the next time unless you do it manually." If I'm not careful and I take too long for this story it will turn into a THOUGHT, a dirty thought. Too late.

BE CAREFUL WHAT YOU SAY

My girlfriends X husband needed a drive to town to get his computer looked at. He was having trouble with it. We had been friends and dart partners. So I offered to drive him to his friends place to get him to look at it. When we got there, now my girlfriends X doesn't always speak clearly, so when he introduced me, what he meant to say was this is my x-wife's boyfriend, but what came out was, "This is my boyfriend." And that's what I heard. Now John looked at me funny and I said, "No, I'm not his boyfriend." And John said, "I'm not here to judge." I said, "I'm his X-wife's boyfriend." I'm not sure if that sounded any better. Everything went silent and we started talking about his computer.

I GET HIGH ON LADDERS

I was talking to this guy who was complaining about all these contractors who were stealing jobs from him. He said, "Everybody and his brother thinks he can be a contractor because they own a ladder." So I said, "I take it you have a ladder too."

NAKED CHICKEN

My grandmother told me this story a long time ago. My father and my uncle where behind the chicken coop and they had a bottle of rum. As they started drinking they thought they heard their mother coming so they threw the bottle into the chicken coop and ran. A couple hours later my grandmother went in to the chicken coop to collect eggs and she found what she thought was a dead chicken. It was still warm, so it was still eatable so she proceeded to pluck it. When she finished the chicken jumped off her lap and ran off. The chicken was just coming off a bender. The moral of the story is, if you get drunk don't turn your back on your mother. There are consequences.

GIVE ME A BREAK

Remember during the time of the pandemic? Of course you remember, that was a dumb question. Anyway, one day I was walking into the Co-op and I was walking by someone I knew and he said Hi Emile. Now that puzzled me. I had a mask on and I had my sunglasses on. How did he know it was me? Superman puts a pair of plain (not prescription) glasses on and nobody knows who he is. Hasn't that ever bothered you?

PICTURE THIS

Me: Seri, can you show me a picture of you?

Seri: Sorry, I left my selfie stick home.

Me: That's funny.

Seri: I'll take that as a compliment.

POEMS

The things we do

A tender touch
A warm embrace
The things we do
To reach that place
A nice warm smile
That special look
The things we do
Could fill a book
A look of love
One single rose
The things we do
That's why love grows
What really makes us
Stand apart
It's the things we do
To reach the heart

U2

WHEN U2 MET
U2 LET
YOUR HEARTS BE JOINED
TOGETHER
WHEN U2 WED
U2 SAID
YOU'D LIVE AND LOVE
FOREVER
IT'S BEEN ONE YEAR
SINCE U2 WED
WHEN WE SEE U2
TOGETHER
IT'S NOT SO HARD
TO UNDERSTAND
WHY U2 SAID
FOREVER

Loving Parents

In all the world, it's not so rare
To find two people who really care,
But what makes you two stand out so much
Is that you affect all the lives you touch.
You give your love, you give your time.
You'd even give your last dime.
I know there is nothing you wouldn't do,
That's just the way you are, you too.
I can't think of any father or mother,
Who love as much as you love each other.
I think you two were meant to be,
As anyone can plainly see.
You've been together all these years,
You've shared many joys and even some tears.
And through the good times and the bad,
You had each other and aren't you glad.
It must have been hard to care for us all,
But you did it and you stood tall.
We've had some good times and some bad'
But we had each other, now, aren't we glad.

Tomorrow

Tomorrow is nothing like today,
Nor is it like yesterday.
You'll always have endless years,
And with it you will have no tears.
Only God knows who will have tomorrow,
A time when there will be no sorrow,
Even if you cry today
Tomorrow won't change in any way.
Even though your hope is strong,
To shed a tear would not be wrong.
Even Jesus broke down and cried
When his good friend Lazarus died.
So take comfort in what you know,
About tomorrow and let them flow
Tears of joy, not sorrow,
Because you always have tomorrow.

ABOUT THE AUTHOR

Born September 26,1948 in Shediac, New Brunswick, Canada. When I started drumming I didn't know I could. When I started playing guitar I didn't know I could. The first time I made love I didn't know. Well I didn't know, someone had to show me. When I started singing I didn't know I could. Now I'm writing. Who'd a thunk.

I started writing this book in 2021 about the same time The Corona Virus started and I had just retired and I didn't know what to do with my life. Hence this book. I like playing the guitar and drums and singing karaoke. My biggest fan is me. I am hansom and humble. The two H's. Don't judge me, but you can if you want to. I love writing, this is *fun, fun, fun*. I like Bud Light and Red Wine. I'm a very decisive person, I think. What can I say about myself that hasn't ever been said before or ever will be. If I don't say it, who will?

This is a quote from when I was young. "I love myself, I think I'm grand, when I'm alone I hold my hand." But only during meditation. Doing it all the time would be just weird and hard to type.

I had two parents, I also have two brothers and one sister. When I was born they didn't break the mold. I would write more about myself but I would probably loose the people who hate to read. If I haven't already. I don't know whats next but I'm ready.

— Emile (*that's all she wrote*) Fougere

Made in United States
North Haven, CT
06 July 2024